INFILTRATING HEALTHCARE

Infiltrating Healthcare

How Marketing
Works Underground
to Influence Nurses

QUINN GRUNDY

Johns Hopkins University Press | *Baltimore*

Printed in the United States of America on acid-free paper
9 8 7 6 5 4 3 2 1

Johns Hopkins University Press
2715 North Charles Street
Baltimore, Maryland 21218-4363
www.press.jhu.edu

Library of Congress Cataloging-in-Publication Data

Names: Grundy, Quinn, 1986– author.
Title: Infiltrating healthcare : how marketing works underground to influence nurses /
  Quinn Grundy.
Description: Baltimore : Johns Hopkins University Press, 2018. | Includes bibliographical
  references and index.
Identifiers: LCCN 2018004457 | ISBN 9781421426754 (hardcover : alk. paper) | ISBN
  9781421426761 (electronic) | ISBN 1421426757 (hardcover : alk. paper) | ISBN 1421426765
  (electronic)
Subjects: | MESH: Nursing | Marketing of Health Services | Nurse's Role | Practice
  Patterns, Nurses' | Drug Industry—economics | Conflict of Interest
Classification: LCC RT86.7 | NLM WY 16.1 | DDC 610.7306/9—dc23
  LC record available at https://lccn.loc.gov/2018004457

A catalog record for this book is available from the British Library.

*Special discounts are available for bulk purchases of this book. For more information,
please contact Special Sales at 410-516-6936 or specialsales@press.jhu.edu.*

Johns Hopkins University Press uses environmentally friendly book materials,
including recycled text paper that is composed of at least 30 percent post-consumer
waste, whenever possible.

CONTENTS

ACKNOWLEDGMENTS

I would first like to thank the research participants who generously gave their time and stories to this project. I also gratefully acknowledge those individuals who took an interest in the project and assisted me in gaining access to their institutions and promoting the project within.

This research was funded by a Graduate Dean's Health Science Fellowship from the University of California, San Francisco, a Doctoral Research Award from the Canadian Institutes of Health Research (CIHR), and grant number R36HS022383 from the Agency for Healthcare Research and Quality. While writing this book, I was supported by a Postdoctoral Fellowship from the CIHR.

I undertook this project with the unparalleled mentorship of Ruth Malone and Lisa Bero. I have benefited immensely from their intellectual and personal generosity and cannot thank them enough for the opportunities they have afforded me.

I am thankful to Shannon Smith-Bernardin and Tae-Wol Stanley and all of my colleagues at the San Francisco Medical Respite and Sobering Center. Shannon and Tae-Wol gave me the opportunity to become a nurse; I gratefully acknowledge the incredible support and flexibility that they allowed me while I conducted this research.

I have enjoyed the support of colleagues, now friends, who have created such stimulating and collaborative working environments throughout this project. I would like to thank Leslie Dubbin, Susan Forsyth, Kate Horton, and Sonia Rab Alam, for their critical contributions to this analysis and their coffee shop and library companionship; Nicholas Chartres, Alice Fabbri, Barbara Mintzes, Darryl Stelmach, and Jeff Wang, for their support through the writing phase; and Alan Cassels, Ellen Goldstein, Annemarie Jutel, Joel Lexchin, Wendy Lipworth, Ray Moynihan, and Marion Nestle, who so generously gave their time to shepherd me through the book-writing process.

I am indebted to my early and thorough readers for their astute insights and careful editing and wish to thank, in particular, Todd Carnam, Mollie James, and Kathy Williams. Thanks to Robin W. Coleman, Barbara Lamb, Laura Williamson, and Katherine Van Zyderveld for their editing services.

My life is blessed by the stalwart friendship of some exceptional people who saw me through the years of this project and have made this time such fun. I wish to thank Virginia and David Blackman, Scott Brunsdon and Lisa Hoelzl, Todd Carnam, Kristopher Geda and Andy Jih, Emily Green, Fabian Held and Adam McGowan, Lea Hermann, Kate Horton, Emilia Patrick, Louise Pocock, Mark and Helena Read, and JP Whan.

I thank my family for their love, support, and encouragement: my parents, Lorie and Paul Grundy; my parents-in-law, Kathy and Lorris Williams; and my sisters, Hayley Grundy, Mollie James, and Grace Grundy. Your FaceTimes, visits, and mountain oases provided much-needed respite and motivation.

Finally, I would like to thank Walter, who arrived right on time, and my husband, Lorris Williams, who quite literally fueled this adventure, and whom I thank for everything.

INFILTRATING HEALTHCARE

Prologue

There is a hush over the hospital at 7 in the morning. Bleary-eyed, anxious family members wave to their fathers, sisters, wives, sons as they are pushed through the double doors marked "restricted access" on their way to surgery. Then they go off to find a coffee or a corner of the waiting room, and proceed to wait. A quiet hum begins to grow; in the locker rooms, the night shift staff peel off their hats, booties, and pale green scrubs, transforming back into regular people, while the day shift performs the opposite transformation. And among this tidal change of greens, there are flashes of bright red scrubs: the medical device sales representatives who pass through the double doors, towing suitcases on wheels, stopping to check in at the nursing station.

In an operating room, a scrub nurse begins setting up her sterile field for a spine surgery. The circulating nurse bustles around, fetching packages of dressings and implements, collecting documents, setting up the electronic chart. Talking among themselves, the nurses chat over the tables as the scrub nurse sets out the tools and supplies they will need in the course of the surgery. Bantering, with notes of irony and humor in their voices, the scrub nurse observes, "This surgeon doesn't like me," while the other offers, "Well, we're not the A-team he prefers," both anticipating conflict of some sort during the case. In walks a tall, blond, good-looking man in bright red scrubs, who greets the nurses warmly. He is the sales representative for the device company that manufactures the screws that will be implanted in the patient's spine during today's surgery.

Andrew, the sales representative, had left his house at 5:30 that morning, hopped in his mobile office (the company car), and commuted to the hospital, one of the biggest clients in his territory. He is there several days a week supporting cases and knows his way around. He has two small children, but puts in 60-plus hours a week, as he works on 100% commission in this "sink or swim" field, as he describes it. He steps out briefly to grab a coffee while the nurse goes to scrub in—a thorough hand and arm washing—and by the time he returns, the scrub nurse is in need of assistance to tie her sterile gown, so he readily sets down the coffee by the charting station to assist. The patient is wheeled into the room by the anesthesia team. The surgical fellow arrives after scrubbing in, greets Andrew warmly, and then hovers over the patient to begin readying for the case. Andrew is not meant to touch anything, so he is exempt from the hand-washing procedure.

Andrew and the scrub nurse stand over the tables covered in supplies and big metal boxes. These are sterile trays filled with tools that look like hammers, screw drivers, clamps, and ratchets, on loan from Andrew's company and included in the price of the screw implants. Andrew's role is to support the scrub nurse; for each case, only about 25% of all the tools they have ready will be used, and these are tailored to the individual surgeon and the case. Although the nurses are orthopedic specialists and have probably worked with these sets of instruments before, spine implants are a highly competitive field. This scrub nurse has likely worked with 10 different surgical sets from various companies, with various surgeons, since she last used these particular tools. Andrew's role is to help the nurse navigate the boxes and have the appropriate tool ready at the appropriate time, helping the nurse set up the equipment and offering suggestions minute to minute during the case. Andrew has a bachelor of science degree in marketing and spent an intensive two weeks at his company's headquarters studying anatomy, the equipment, and sales strategies, followed by six months of field training with an experienced sales representative. Occasionally, Andrew perceives that nurses resent this help, as he has no clinical training, but ignoring his suggestions could mean slowing down the surgery and angering the surgeon.

As the surgical fellow (junior surgeon) begins the case, draping the patient and sterilizing the skin, Andrew attempts to make himself useful. He answers the phone when it rings—"Hello? OR #1, this is Andrew"; he picks up the packaging the scrub nurse discards from her sterile field; he banters with the techs; when the OR tech brings in a missing item, he praises him, "You're the best!"

The surgeon then arrives and introduces himself to those in the room. He has an air of celebrity and is accompanied by two international visiting surgeons. Andrew has known this surgeon for more than six years and praises him as "incredibly talented . . . I don't want to say, 'fast,' but he is very efficient and does procedures in a quarter of the time it takes others." Andrew recently accompanied this surgeon, at the surgeon's request, on an international trip to complete a "high-profile case on a rich business man"; his company and the surgeon shared the cost of his trip. The surgeon brought Andrew along to work with the nurses during the case.

After orienting himself, the surgeon barks at a surgical technician regarding a missing implement and at the X-ray tech because the X-ray machine is not immediately available. Andrew gives the OR tech a comforting pat on the back when the surgeon's back is turned.

The procedure commences: the surgeon standing over the patient, the scrub nurse just a few feet to his side, presiding over the sterile field, while Andrew is just on the other side, monitoring their every move. At this stage, Andrew quietly tells the scrub nurse to get certain tools ready, to trade an implement for one of another size, and then, to show the surgeon the allograft "now." She seems reassured by his presence, responding to his suggestions instantly. The interaction between Andrew and the nurse falls into even greater sync when a ratchet malfunctions as the pace of the surgery picks up. The surgeon is feeling pressured—at this stage the implants are being placed—and in turn, pressures the scrub nurse; time is of the essence. Implements fall more heavily on her table as if tossed or dropped, the tools themselves sounding frustrated. At one point the surgeon makes a sharp remark to the nurse, who does not respond except to raise her eyebrows to the circulating nurse when the surgeon's back is turned. The intensity of the case escalating, the surgeon continues to show impatience with the nurse and to give curt orders, in response to which she turns to Andrew, who readily provides direction. In concert, they do their best to avoid an eruption of the surgeon's anger, to deescalate his impatience. In this way, Andrew—an expert in this surgeon's particularities, idiosyncrasies, temperament, technique, and preferences—acts as a translator and mediator for the nurse, helping to avoid the abuse that is both unpleasant and stressful, but also potentially dangerous when a patient's spine lies exposed on the operating table.

By the end of the case, four little screws are in the patient's spine. The patient is wheeled out of the room to the recovery area, accompanied by the circulating nurse, who completes the handover to the postoperative team. The surgical fellow goes to clean the blood off his shoes, which had soaked through his shoe covers, before speaking with the family; the scrub nurse to reorganize the equipment for sterile processing and to complete the documentation. Andrew pulls out an iPad, asking the nurse to double-check the itemized implants, and submits the invoice for the screws to the company and the hospital billing department—a total of several thousand dollars. It is not yet noon. Andrew says his good-byes and takes off, heading back to his mobile office to catch up on emails and calls before he heads to another hospital and another case.

chapter 1

Invisible Influence

Marketing and the Most Trusted Profession

Soon after the initial release of the Open Payments data in the United States, a team of investigative journalists at ProPublica, a nonprofit news organization, dug into the data. They found that more than 14,600 physicians had received gifts or payments from pharmaceutical or medical device companies on 100 days or more in the course of 2014.[1] A handful of physicians had accepted company payments, gifts, meals, or drinks on more days of the year than not.[1] Sales representatives were embedded in these medical practices, with daily sales calls accompanied by free samples, lunches, and invitations to the clinicians to give talks or travel to conferences.

This data, published by the Centers for Medicare & Medicaid Services on the Open Payments website, shows how pervasive the presence of pharmaceutical and medical device companies within medical practice has become. Tucked into the massive Affordable Care Act, the healthcare reform legislation passed by the Obama administration, the Physician Payments Sunshine Act mandated that pharmaceutical and medical device companies whose products are covered by public insurance programs publicly report all payments to physicians and teaching hospitals valued at more than $10.[2] Members of the public can now look up their doctor on the Open Payments database and see the number, type, value and source of any payments their doctor received from drug or device companies (https://openpaymentsdata.cms.gov/). Since 2013, some 906,000 physicians have received 38.23 million payments, valued at $6.99 billion, from 2,078 different companies.[3]

Senator Charles Grassley first introduced the bill in 2007 after the *New York Times* reported on the growing prescription of antipsychotic drugs to children and the sometimes severe side effects.[4] The *Times* also reported that a child psychiatrist who had written a highly influential research study about the use of atypical antipsychotics, a new class of medications, had been paid $180,000 from two manufacturers of these drugs.[4] When the journalists inquired, the psychiatrist had responded, "Trust me, I don't make much."[4] This greatly troubled Grassley and his staffers.[5] Trust was exactly the problem—why couldn't doctors be held at least to the same minimal disclosure standards as elected officials?

This sunshine legislation wasn't new—several states already had transparency legislation and even bans on health professionals receiving gifts from companies—but Grassley's bill would now cover all physicians in the United States. In his introductory speech to the Senate, Grassley stated, "Companies wouldn't be paying this money unless it had a direct effect on the prescriptions doctors write, and the medical devices they use. Patients, of course, are in the dark about whether their doctor is receiving this money." The legislation wasn't designed to regulate business, Grassley explained, and it didn't limit any kind of relationship between physicians and companies. For Grassley, the aim was to "let a little bit of sunshine in to this world of financial relationships—it is, after all, the best disinfectant."[6]

While there is little evidence that the publication of this data has had a disinfecting effect—the number and nature of payments from industry to physicians hasn't really changed, though it may be too early to tell[7]—it has allowed researchers and journalists to paint a clearer picture of industry influence over patient care. A growing number of studies has found that physicians who accept gifts and payments from pharmaceutical and medical device companies are significantly more likely to prescribe high-cost, brand name, heavily marketed treatments.[8-11] And it only takes a sandwich: researchers found that physicians were more likely to prescribe a promoted drug if they received a single meal, which cost on average only $12 to $18.[8]

These new, often heavily marketed medicines and devices are more likely to be recalled or accompanied by a black box warning, designed to alert prescribers to serious or life-threatening safety issues, than generic drugs or those that have been on the market for several years.[12] Because clinical trials are performed for short periods of time and are often restricted to relatively healthy volunteers, serious side effects may not become apparent until a drug is on the market and has been widely used by people with multiple conditions or on multiple medications. This happened with Vioxx (rofecoxib), which turned out to carry increased risk of heart attack and stroke, causing Merck, the manufacturer, to pull it from the market, but only after tens of thousands of people had suffered or died from serious heart disease.[13]

The pharmaceutical industry spends nearly $71 billion a year on marketing,[14] nearly twice the amount the industry spends on research and development.[15] More than one-third of this money is spent on visits to health professionals by sales representatives, suggesting that promotion to health professionals is a priority for the pharmaceutical industry.[15] Sales representatives are often the most common source of drug information for prescribers.[16-18] The trouble is that this information is often highly biased: sales representatives provided a minimally adequate amount of safety information in only 1.7% of all sales visits to primary care physicians in a study in the United States, Canada, and France.[19] Instead, the drug's health benefits were described twice as often, and in more than half the visits, sales representatives failed to mention a single harmful effect. Whistleblower complaints and internal industry documents made public through litigation have revealed that the purpose behind visits to health professionals is to increase the sale of a drug, often through illegal practices such as promoting off-label uses.[20-22] Drug regulators approve medicines for specific uses for which there are studies showing that the drug is effective and safe. Promoting off-label use is illegal because when a drug has not been tested for a particular purpose, regulators can't know if it is safe to use or will work for that purpose.[21]

For example, in 2004, Warner-Lambert, a subsidiary of Pfizer, pled guilty and agreed to pay fines of $430 million for promoting the drug gabapentin during the 1990s for uses that were not approved by the US Food and Drug Administration.[22] The internal company documents that were made public during these legal proceedings detailed a $40 million multipronged strategy to promote the use of gabapentin. The company recruited local champions of the drug to serve as speakers in peer selling programs.[22] Physicians known to be high prescribers of anticonvulsants (an off-label use for gabapentin) were invited to serve as consultants. During these meetings, "hard-hitting" messages about the promoted drug were delivered.[22] Educational events were a company priority; teleconferences were organized for physicians in which a clinical leader would deliver a talk designed to persuade nonprescribers to begin prescribing gabapentin and current prescribers to increase the number of prescriptions they wrote. Finally, the company created research opportunities for influential physicians, funding small studies about the promoted drug.[22]

The sheer number and size of high-profile recent settlements between the federal United States government and pharmaceutical companies for alleged illegal marketing practices suggest that these practices are pervasive and that settlement costs have become merely part of the cost of doing business.[21] The hidden costs, however, are a public burden. The public pays for these practices not only through sky-rocketing drug prices but also with their health when exposed to drug-induced side effects, sometimes resulting in disability or death.[13] Opioid overdose is now the leading cause of death for people under the age of 50 in the United States,[23] a public health crisis linked closely to the aggressive promotion of prescription painkillers by pharmaceutical companies like Purdue Pharma, which misled health professionals and patients about the dangers of addiction.[24]

The focus of all this scrutiny, however, has remained squarely on physicians. Nurses, who represent the largest proportion of health professionals, are omitted from the Physician Payments Sunshine

Act, and almost nothing is known about nurses' interactions with industry.[25,26] The Sunshine Act originally included physicians and teaching hospitals, as well as podiatrists, dentists, chiropractors, optometrists, and osteopaths. Senator Grassley introduced a new bill to the US Senate in 2015 to close a loophole in the original Sunshine Act by including nurse prescribers, physician assistants, and some prescribing pharmacists, but it hasn't moved past the Senate Finance Committee.[27]

What about the 3 million registered nurses who do not prescribe? Registered nurses are the largest group of health professionals, making up 34% of the population of health professionals in the United States.[28] Members of one of the fastest-growing professions, registered nurses are present in just about every healthcare setting. Registered nurses are represented at all levels of institutional hierarchy, from the bedside to the executive suite, and they practice in diverse capacities, including direct patient care, hospital administration, nursing education, case management, quality improvement, research, and policy making.

As more countries adopt their own version of the Sunshine Act, however, the omission of nurses from the US transparency laws truly looks like an oversight. For example, in Australia, nurses attended nearly 40% of the 116,845 pharmaceutical industry-sponsored events over a four-year period, which was nearly twice as often as primary care physicians.[29] The pharmaceutical industry appears to be highly inclusive of multiple health professionals when it comes to marketing.

The glaring omission of registered nurses from policies and literature about industry influence on healthcare made me ask: Are policy makers unaware that nurses interact with industry in much the same way that physicians do? Or, do they not believe these interactions are important enough to warrant regulation?

This book is the culmination of a two-year investigation into the routine, yet influential ways that registered nurses interact with sales representatives of medically related companies in the course of day-to-day clinical practice. Nurses working in acute care hospitals in the United States interact with sales representatives from what I call "medically related industry," consisting of not only the pharmaceutical and medical device industries but also medical equipment, nutrition and infant formula, and health technology companies.

My research into these relationships revealed that, as policy makers focus on physicians, nurses increasingly interact with sales representatives on a daily basis. The medically related industry has found the perfect partner in the registered nurse, whose work is largely invisible yet who wields a great deal of influence over treatment and purchasing decisions, much of it unrecognized.

"Just" a Nurse

When Kelley Johnson took to the stage during the talent portion of the 2015 Miss America pageant, she took the audience by surprise. Instead of the anticipated glitz and glamor typical of the opera arias, ballet dancing, and magic tricks, Kelley Johnson, as Miss Colorado, wore scrubs, her hair in a ponytail and a stethoscope around her neck. She delivered a monologue wherein she asserted that she was "never going to be just a nurse," sharing her story of caring for a patient, Joe, in the early stages of Alzheimer's disease.[30] In his suffering, she expertly cared for Joe, but met his pleas for a change in his treatments or to fix his medications with, "No, Joe. I can't, I'm just a nurse." During a particularly difficult night, when her words provided comfort, Joe countered, "Although you say it all the time, you are not just a nurse. You are my nurse." The next day, hosts on *The View* mocked this performance and questioned why she was wearing a "doctor's stethoscope."[31] Her monologue and the ensuing criticism triggered a media storm. Nurses, in a show of support, flooded social media with photos of themselves using their stethoscopes, suggesting that many nurses are all too familiar with being regarded by society as "just a nurse."

The omission of nurses from the Sunshine Act may speak to a similar phenomenon, the myth that "just" nurses do not make decisions in the absence of "doctor's orders." Through the course of my research, I frequently came up against similar deeply held assumptions about the role of nurses in hospitals, including the assumption that nurses do not typically interact with industry.

In reality, the registered nurse is arguably the most important clinician for medically related industries in this era of health reform, situated at the hub of multidisciplinary teams and focused on the prevention and management of increasingly common and costly chronic diseases.[32] In light of increased restrictions on sales representatives' access to physicians, nurses have increasingly become a "soft target" for industry's promotional activities.[33] By forming relationships with nurses, the for-profit medically related industry gains unprecedented behind-the-scenes access to and influence over decisions from the bedside to the hospital boardroom.

Although nurses have also become a marketing target in their own right, their influence over treatment and purchasing decisions in hospitals remains largely invisible to policy makers and unknown to the general public. Nurses have unique and direct 24/7 access to patients and prescribers. Despite lacking the authority to prescribe, nurses frequently influence treatment decisions by recommending medications to patients and prescribers and providing feedback on treatment outcomes.[34] Nurses play a vital role in medication adherence, ensuring that prescriptions get filled and refilled. This is of great interest to pharamceutical companies, which must not only increase the number of prescriptions written but, especially for chronic conditions, must also ensure that prescriptions are refilled as often as possible and that the time between identifying a condition and getting a prescription to treat it is as short as possible.[35]

Nurse managers oversee large departmental operating budgets for medical supplies, pharmacy stock, and equipment rentals. Nurses play key roles in researching, evaluating, and selecting the medical products, devices, and equipment a hospital must purchase. The Association of periOperative Registered Nurses hosts an annual Surgical Conference and Expo. In the marketing prospectus delivered to potential exhibitors, the conference organizers advertised that "71.6% of attendees influence purchasing at their facilities. 45% recommend new products. 25% are part of a purchasing/evaluation committee." Hospitals are increasingly implementing formal purchasing committees, known by a variety of names, including "value analysis," "product evaluation," or "value-added committees," which bring together supply chain professionals and clinicians, usually nurses, to make decisions about devices, equipment, and supplies. Hospitals spend up to 40% of their budgets on supplies, equipment, and housekeeping, costs that grew by 35% to 40% in the 2000s.[36] With these cost pressures, hospitals are looking for ways to save money on devices and equipment without compromising the quality or safety of patient care. One way to do this is to have nurses work closely with the supply chain department to formally evaluate every new product that the hospital might want to purchase—to have people at the table who can say whether a new product truly represents an advance in practice or that what has been brought to the table is largely a product of hype.[37]

Nurses' influence over treatment and purchasing decisions has been largely overlooked. Similarly, the marketing activities of the medical device industry, as well as health information technology, nutrition (including infant formula), and other medically related industries, have been given little attention compared with the pharmaceutical industry. Yet, these companies market products that come into direct contact with patients and, collectively, account for an enormous cost.

The Research

Over the course of two years investigating the nature of interactions between registered nurses and medically related industry in clinical practice, I followed nurses into operating rooms, purchasing committee meetings, and onto patient care units at four hospitals in the metropolitan area of a large western US city.

I met the sales representatives with whom the nurses worked on a daily basis in the places where nurses were caring for patients. I had not known that sales representatives, working largely on commission, are assisting in operating rooms for the duration of a surgery, helping set up the equipment and advising the nurses and surgeons on the selection and use of the devices. Other sales representatives permitted me to shadow them as they roamed patient care units, delivering five-minute in-service education on a new gown or glucometer and handing out candy in exchange for a nurse's time.

I collected stories of encounters with industry from staff nurses working at the bedside and from nurse administrators running departments. I attended the circus-like Critical Care Expo—an industry trade show held in conjunction with a professional conference attended by more than 8,000 nurses—where I collected a suitcase full of marketing brochures, free samples, and squishy eyeball stress balls and ate sponsored meal after sponsored meal.

This book, the result of that research, is the first account of nurses' perspectives on the ways that the industry's marketing practices have become a routine part of the delivery of healthcare. Unless I have cited an additional source, all the stories shared here were drawn from interviews or direct observations, with verbatim quotations edited only to eliminate filler words and to shield the identity of particular persons and organizations. To protect the identities of those who shared their experiences, I have used pseudonyms throughout the book and have not identified the hospitals where these nurses worked.

"It Doesn't Happen Here"

When I first approached administrators to request access to their hospitals to conduct this research, I was repeatedly told that interactions between nurses and industry "didn't happen." Administrators explained that their hospital had a policy that prevented sales representatives from dropping in and also that nurses really didn't have reason to be meeting with industry.

A colleague had put me in touch with a nurse who ran a department of electrophysiology—sometimes called the "cath" lab, where patients go for procedures on their heart that are done via a catheter instead of through surgery. This nurse director was eager to have me observe the daily interactions between the staff nurses in her department and the sales reps from the companies that make pacemakers. Every time a patient was having a pacemaker put in or deactivated, the sales rep would be present, alongside the nurses and doctors. But when she took the request for my visit to the vice president of nursing, the answer was no. The vice president replied, "Our nurses and managers do not interact with vendors," a commonly used term for industry representatives. "If a vendor is asked to present it is done in a structured committee. The only interaction our nurses and managers would have is with the in-service arm of a company we have purchased a new product from."

Despite asserting that the nurses "do not interact with vendors," this administrator also said that nurses *did* sit on purchasing committees, where sales reps presented their products. She also explained that industry representatives provided training to staff nurses about new products the hospital had purchased in the form of an in-service. These are typically 5- to 10-minute demonstrations that sales representatives perform on the patient care units while nurses are working, though they are sometimes more extensive and involve lunch-hour or half-day trainings.

But somehow, to the vice president, the in-services and committee meetings didn't count as nurses interacting with industry. And the day-to-day interactions between the nurses and the pacemaker reps, which included contacting the device rep to alert them that a patient was coming in, getting the rep through the door with a proper ID badge and paperwork, coordinating with the rep regarding the patient's condition and needs, and facilitating the sales rep's contact with the patient, were not mentioned at all. This made me think that there might be much more going on.

A number of other administrators I approached suggested that I try a hospital that didn't have a formal policy. Academic medical centers, in particular, have largely adopted some kind of conflict of interest policy, which may also restrict sales reps' access to physicians, students, or staff.[38] Many pointed to the advent of these policies as the point at which the lavishness of industry sponsorship was curbed, recalling the days of all-expenses-paid golf trips to Hawaii or gifts of Rolex watches for eminent physicians.

In contrast to administrators' belief that "it doesn't happen here," the reality could not have been more different. For many of the nurses I interviewed, interacting with sales representatives was built into their very jobs. Often they could not accomplish their work without the information, personnel, or financial support that sales representatives provided. One nurse explained, "Nurses have been involved for *years* . . . We interact [with industry] very heavily." She elaborated, saying, "So nurses for decades in the operating room have been tagged as the 'money-managers,' and you can talk to a surgeon all you want, but if you want to get something in the operating room you better be talking to the nurse in charge."

However invisible these workday interactions were to hospital administrators and policy makers, nurses' interactions with the medical industry outside of the workplace were even less visible. For example, many nurses I interviewed had attended drug company-sponsored dinners, and some had served as paid speakers for sponsoring companies. Many acknowledged that their employers had no knowledge of these financial relationships external to their jobs, and some felt entitled to attend sponsored events "on their own time," believing they could detect and separate marketing influence from their clinical responsibilities.

One administrator understood, however, the interest that industry had in nurses and the impact nurses had on hospital budgets. He was the director of materials, in charge of a multimillion-dollar budget for supplies and equipment. "And so all these sales things were happening, traditionally, and a lot of literature on how it's marketed to physicians," he reflected. "But here it happens tremendously to nurses, because the nurses are on the front line: (a) they're here all the time and accessible; (b) they're dealing with the patient directly; and (c) they're the ones that sit on the purchasing committee." Nurses were omnipresent in the hospital across all clinical areas, but they also had direct contact with those who were industry's ultimate consumers—prescribers, purchasers, and patients.

In the place of making sales calls, many companies have repositioned themselves to offer what they deem "education." Through providing product support in clinical settings, sales representatives increasingly work alongside nurses as product experts. Although their function remains primarily sales, their clinical presence blurs the boundaries between patient care and medical sales.

I show that under the guise of "education" or product "support," sales representatives partner with nurses, members of the "most trusted" profession,[39] and capitalize on their credibility. In these ways, sales representatives secure an "inside man," as one nurse put it, in the hospital. Through the offers of gifts, samples, and a helping hand, sales representatives secure nurses as allies in promoting their products throughout the hospital. They are thus able to introduce high-cost brand name products and equipment that may be backed up by little evidence of safety or efficacy into routine patient care.

Moreover, they are able to do so with minimal oversight. I explore why marketing to nurses has been overlooked by policy makers through tracing deeply held assumptions about the nature of nurses' work, namely, that because nurses do not prescribe, they have no influence on treatment decisions. This misconception casts marketing drugs and devices to nurses as benign, given the perception that there is no decision for marketing to sway. Thus, interactions between nurses and industry are subject to little scrutiny.

Why This Matters

One nurse who worked in the operating room called herself the "compliance person guardian angel" and was known by less nice names for throwing out cookies brought in by sales representatives, chastising colleagues for partaking in free dinners, and confronting aggressive sales representatives. She willingly took the flak because she saw the nurse as a patient's last line of defense. "Unlike all the area of the hospital," she explained,

> there are no family visitors in [the operating room]. There's no one who can come, and there's no one who can make sure that these people are okay. And the vendors aren't worried about the patients. The vendors are worried about selling the product. That's truly what they are. They're businessmen. And the doctors are worried about doing a good case—doing good surgery, making sure the patient's doing okay. The vendor is there to support them in doing that.

As sales representatives become embedded in day-to-day clinical practice, their marketing function is obscured. By partnering with nurses, sales representatives become credible and legitimate members of the healthcare team. However, these reps, working on commission, are highly incentivized to push the sale of their products. The healthcare system is left to cope with spiraling costs for devices and equipment, problems of overtreatment and overdiagnosis, and an epidemic of adverse drug reactions. The public needs to trust that nurses—their advocates—are making crucial decisions free from commercial influence and know when the line between service and sales is crossed.

I am calling for a new moral space within healthcare—one in which all health professionals, including nurses, physicians, pharmacists, and allied health professionals, can work with industry without putting patients, hospital budgets, or their own decision making at risk. This will require bringing the mundane, but highly influential relationships between nurses and industry to light. It requires that we take a stand on marketing in clinical spaces and collectively agree that health professionals do not need donuts or branded pens to do their work. It also means that we need to demand independent information for clinical training, continuing education, purchasing, and patient support and truly separate sales from product support.

This book is a call to action to protect the clinical spaces where we are at our most vulnerable, and the decisions that take place there, from the pursuit of profit at any cost.

Overview

Hospitals increasingly rely on industry to keep up with technological developments and support the use of products in practice. Many hospitals have instituted formal policies and procedures around industry interactions to prevent exposure to risk and to control costs associated with the purchase of equipment and supplies. These kinds of formal structure were often the first topic of discussion in the interviews I conducted. Nurse managers stressed that "we don't take cold calls" and pointed to the implementation of various policies that they perceived had dramatically decreased the frequency of sales interactions. Many others suggested that regulations had "tightened up" the nature of interactions with industry and that administrators had ultimately "made sure that vendors weren't having any influence." However, for the remainder of these interviews, participants would recount numerous, richly detailed narratives about their day-to-day interactions with company representatives who worked in a sales capacity.

In Chapter 2, "From Sales to Service," I explore the processes by which certain interactions between nurses and sales representatives have been transformed into a service experience, obscuring the shared sales function. Thus, hospital administrators have allowed such interactions to be effectively built into the normal, and vital, day-to-day functioning of the hospital.

While attempting to neutralize marketing influence, hospitals' formal policies also serve to obscure the fact that nurses' interactions with industry are also a marketing opportunity. Chapter 2 explores three commonly occurring contexts for interactions between nurses and sales representatives—sales visits, purchasing committees, and contracted in-service education—and shows how marketing activities have been transformed into routine institutional practices.

The result is that nurses and administrators perceive many day-to-day industry interactions as something other than a marketing encounter, and thus these interactions are not subject to the same scrutiny or oversight as those that remain under the umbrella of marketing. These formal structures have instead blended marketing interactions with other institutional activities in such a way as to make the goals of industry and the hospital appear aligned. Consequently, industry representatives have become a "local species," in the words of one nurse, formally classified as belonging, as denoted by their hospital badges, and informally as a day-to-day presence.

On the frontlines of clinical practice, nurses juggle multiple patients, physicians, families, managers, and the real-world constraints of never having enough time or resources. In the middle of this balancing act steps the sales representative, who readily offers a helping hand, but also camaraderie, offers to go to lunch, and donuts for the staff meeting—"The Perfect Friend." In Chapter 3, I show how sales reps also employ a host of informal mechanisms to build relationships with nurses and make themselves indispensable in the day-to-day running of a hospital. Expertly attuned to the realities of nursing practice, this kind of friendship is highly instrumental, and the sales rep becomes a true team player, creating the appearance that nurses' and industry's goals are aligned. However, friendship is a two-way street: nurses also serve as the perfect friends to sales reps because they are trusted insiders with intimate knowledge of the system. Sales reps are able to capitalize on nurses' insider knowledge as a means of more effectively introducing products into the hospital and of ensuring their success among end users.

This instrumental kind of friendship is a different kind of seduction from that in which the pharmaceutical industry wooed physicians with trips to Hawaii and large consulting payments; it validates the importance of nurses' work in a way it has long been systematically denied. Nonetheless, this relationship is powerful and much more insidious in that this type of marketing influence presents itself as a partnership in the name of patient care while still pursuing profit at any expense. And it is a partnership that happens mostly out of sight. Thus, purchasing committees and other decision makers largely had no idea that the representatives of companies whose products were under scrutiny had personal relationships with the nurses promoting them.

During the course of this study, I was often asked, "If nurses do not prescribe, why does marketing to nurses matter?" In Chapter 4, I confront what I call the "as-if" world of nursing practice—the well-constructed, institutionally preserved and defended myth that nurses do not initiate any meaningful activities in the absence of a doctor's order—*as if* they did not make decisions.

I contend that the omission of nurses from recent policies related to the disclosure and management of conflicts of interest is yet another manifestation of the as-if world of nursing practice. This omission functions to sustain the as-if myth in two ways: it appears *as if* nurses who do not prescribe do not interact with industry representatives, and *as if* the potential consequences of marketing influence on nurses' decision making are not of sufficient importance to warrant policy attention.

Surprisingly, many nurses had internalized this myth: though most participants took part in marketing activities such as industry-sponsored dinners, many seemed mystified at the attention from sales representatives. In speaking with nurses, it was apparent that many did not identify as individual decision makers; thus, there was no decision for marketing to sway, and many nurses were puzzled at the dedication of industry resources to nursing audiences. Rather, they described their ability to effect change, to control resources, or to determine practices as having "influence," which apparently did not reconcile with how they believed a decision maker should act.

More specifically, nurses described practicing within hierarchical institutions in which the knowledge, control, and authority they did possess were frequently constrained. I explore the range of nurses' reactions to marketing within this context—some nurses experienced marketing as benign, others as validating. A minority confronted the as-if myth, asserting that nurses were indeed essential patient advocates, and they were vigilant toward marketing influence that could threaten patient well-being.

Despite the frequency and depth of the daily contact between nurses and sales representatives, these interactions are almost entirely invisible to hospital administrators and policy makers. Consequently, the practical and ethical management of interactions with industry is outsourced to individual nurses who navigate this part of their practice on an ad hoc and experiential basis. In Chapter 5, I explore how this minority took a stand against commercial influence in clinical spaces.

"There Are Rules of Engagement" explores the ways in which nurses frame their interactions with industry in moral terms. Few participants explicitly named their interactions with sales representatives as "ethical," but for some, their interactions with industry provoked unease and disquiet. Compelled by "close calls," a few nurses had created personalized "rules of engagement," as one nurse called them, which they enacted in the pursuit of fairness, transparency, and the safety of their patients. Serving as sentinels to marketing influence in their hospitals, these nurses filled in gaps left by formal policy with their individual strategies. These strategies were markedly diverse, enabling sales representatives to tailor their marketing approach to individuals or to work around the corner, undermining these efforts within the hospital.

Some nurses who worked in highly controlled areas such as operating rooms took on policing practices. They had developed these practices to enforce department-specific rules— checking for identification, throwing out sales representatives' food or drinks, filing complaints against particular sales representatives. Others adopted bargaining tactics from the business world, understanding that industry played by different rules; they sought to level the playing field by engaging sales representatives on their own terms. With nurses who approached these interactions skeptically, the gut feeling that industry interactions contained an element of threat was elevated to the level of paranoia. These skeptics perceived every interaction with industry to be morally significant, requiring constant vigilance. This resulted in a heightened sense of ambivalence toward industry interactions because, like others, these nurses were also highly reliant on industry resources.

There were very few nurses who used the language found in policy and research about industry relationships—"conflict of interest," "bias," "disclosure." One participant, Maria—who used the phrase "rules of engagement"—stood out in that she named her interactions with industry explicitly as ethical. Highly attuned to her own negative emotions arising in the course of industry interactions, she set boundaries in the context of these relationships. Maria approached these interactions with great vigilance, safety being her paramount concern, acting as a gatekeeper for sales representatives' access to health professionals and patients.

Sales representatives, through their relationships with nurses, have become a routine and invisible part of healthcare, to the likely detriment of patients and health systems. Paradoxically, policies sustain the invisibility of marketing in clinical spaces because hospital administrators aim to curb marketing influence but still seek to benefit from industry resources.

I conclude by arguing that we can and must work to foster a moral space within healthcare that preserves the promise of innovation and the trust we place in those who care for us when we are at our most vulnerable. I propose a series of vital policy reforms to build a moral climate within healthcare, one that promotes transparency, fosters moral attunement in the context of interactions with industry, and effectively controls marketing influence.

The medically related industry is an important part of healthcare; clinicians could not currently practice without the drugs, devices, equipment, and supplies produced by these companies. My proposed reforms are designed to suggest ways to best work together: to promote developments in the quality and safety of care that are also cost-effective; to base decision making on unbiased information; and to foster transparency and the preservation of public trust.

chapter 2

From Sales to Service

Becoming Strategically Invisible

Before becoming a nurse, Ashley had worked as a waitress at a high-end steakhouse—the kind of restaurant that is so expensive they don't put prices next to menu items. The restaurant's "big thing," she said to me, "is they make a *lot* of money off drug companies and other vendors paying for dinner to make sure that folks were interested in the product." Pharmaceutical companies regularly rented out the restaurant's private dining room and paid specialists to come and give talks to rooms full of doctors and nurses treated to dinners with wine—and a price tag of $200 a head.

She was still working at the restaurant when she was hired as a staff nurse on a transplant unit at a teaching hospital. She was curious to know whether this kind of lavish entertainment was offered to physicians and nurses in a clinical area in which the drugs were really expensive, but necessary to prevent a patient's body from rejecting a new organ. Compared to the wining and dining of doctors by drug companies in an effort to influence which drugs they prescribed, on the transplant unit, she found, the efforts were "dialed down a little bit." Colleagues assured her that this kind of thing didn't happen, and she thought that the hospital had a pretty strict policy in place banning attendance at such events.

"We did still see the drug reps every once in a while, with food and a presentation about effectiveness," she recalled. However, "I think there's a little scratch there that isn't necessarily the one that tickles my ethical bone," she reasoned.

Drug reps would drop Chinese takeout or pizza in the nurses' break room and hang around to chat about the nurses' experiences using their drug, but "it was always kind of with a wink because that was the only drug we had available to fix the problem, and it was the best one on the market." These kinds of interactions were, at worst, an inconvenience. "I never had that feeling of, somebody's pitching me something or selling me something, because at the end of the day, I was going to give that drug," she reflected, "whether or not these people came to talk to us." For Ashley, the little perks like a free lunch didn't serve as a vehicle for marketing influence because, as she pointed out, she would administer the drug the physician had ordered, which was accepted to be the best treatment currently available. Influence could only occur, she believed, when a clinician was faced with the choice of competing products.

Nevertheless, though it seemed to Ashley that she had no other drugs to choose from at the time, pharmaceutical companies often plan their marketing strategies decades in advance, seeking to protect their market share from competitors' products or generic alternatives that will inevitably be introduced down the line. Building brand loyalty with everyone who handles the drug, from the prescriber to the dispenser to the nurse administering it directly to patients, is crucial for market success.[1] Unlike other consumer products, for which consumers make brand choices, there are a number of intermediaries who serve as gatekeepers between drug and device companies and patients, including regulators, insurers, guideline developers, prescribers, and caregivers. Providing a takeout lunch to the staff nurses on a specialty unit is one small part of a complex marketing channel that aims to bring all of these gatekeepers into agreement and make them feel as if they are pursuing the same goal.[1]

For the past four years, Ashley had been knee-deep in the implementation of a new electronic health record at her teaching hospital, working to bring about the massive institutional and cultural shift from paper to electronic records. Seconded out of her clinical role as a staff nurse for the duration of the implementation project, she was one of many nurses working with the company to customize the user interface, coordinate multiple trainings, and provide leadership for the rollout of the new electronic health record in her clinical area.

"I directly worked with some of the company's consultants," she told me, "so vendor folks were on site designing the product and there was interaction in that regard, but it wasn't what I would consider, as a healthcare worker, the *classic* form of interaction."

Instead, her relationships with the industry consultants and sales representatives felt nothing like marketing, but were collaborative, a natural addition to a well-functioning team.

"This time," she reflected, "all this time we're working with [the electronic health record company] has made it a less uncomfortable relationship. There's, again, collaboration. You have to work together to get to the end point."

In this case, Ashley and the company shared the goal of successfully transitioning the entire staff to the new system. She was still working with sales people with sometimes divergent goals—"folks that are selling a product believe in it and are paid to convince you that there's not going to be anything wrong"—so this alignment required, in Ashley's words, "some collaboration."

I spoke with Ashley in her little office in the Nursing Education Department, about a month and a half after she had taken on a nurse educator position. "It's been interesting how much vendors are part of this role," she reflected, referring to sales representatives for medical device and equipment companies with whom she would coordinate staff training in the form of in-services. Unlike the drug dinners, "where it felt a little bit more like advertising," Ashley described her current relationships with sales representatives as "very aboveboard, professional. It's seamlessly so. It's not as if we have to *make* it that way, because generally when they're here, they've already sold the product." She continued, "It's the interaction with someone outside of the hospital and all of that formality, but not necessarily the *influence*, you know?" Unlike the sales reps who would casually stop by the transplant unit with pizza boxes to check in with the nurses on a specialist's request, these interactions had the air of formality as they were contracted through purchasing agreements. They were built into her job and necessary for her work.

In other words, these relationships did not feel like marketing. However, the representatives with whom Ashley interacted in her nurse educator role were largely in sales. Although a few companies have employees in dedicated training roles, several nurse educators perceived, as Ashley did, that many of these positions had been cut. Instead, the sales representative for the product often takes responsibility for the aftercare, following through with product training and support after purchase as part of the sales package. Ensuring that the new product is well known, well liked, and well used among nurses means that the hospital will likely continue to renew, or even increase, its purchasing order.

Ashley acknowledged, "We use a lot of vendor-provided teaching materials . . . The company will send us a bunch of free stuff to do it because they want us to keep buying the product, and the way we keep buying it is having nurses good at using it. Because the time that we look for new products is when people don't find that the current ones are very useable." Because these training-related interactions were formalized and happened after the product had been purchased, nurses questioned the existence of commercial influence. In addition, their shared function as a marketing opportunity was overlooked in the eyes of administrators in the service of accessing industry's resources. This meant that sales representatives could expand the indications for using their products or introduce related ones without coming up against suspicious clinicians or the oversight of administrators. Certain interactions between nurses and industry, like the ones Ashley had regularly in her work as a nurse educator, have undergone a transformation from sales to service. This transformation takes place through the implementation of formal policies and procedures in which the interaction with sales reps becomes a widespread and routine hospital practice. Hospital administrators have brought in these policies to curb the influence of sales reps on doctors and nurses and to reduce the hospital's liability from having sales reps walk in off the street to pitch their products. While these policies set boundaries to what sales reps are permitted to do when in the hospital, they also make interactions between nurses and sales representatives part of business as usual.

Hospitals are highly invested in nurses' interactions with industry and are reliant on industry's resources to perform essential hospital activities. Industry is filling resource gaps for hospitals, particularly in the areas of education and support. In exchange for these resources, sales reps gain legitimacy and credibility as hospital "insiders," manifested in their daily presence in clinical spaces, in markers of inclusion like the identification badge or colored scrubs, and in their status as product and sometimes even practice experts.

Because sales reps are allowed to be in the hospital, their interactions with nurses now appear to be about taking care of patients, which obscures the reality that these interactions are also a marketing opportunity. These interactions become invisible—and strategically so. The invisibility is strategic because hospitals are able to continue to benefit from the resources provided by industry, while passing along the financial, physical, and ethical costs of these interactions to patients and the public. Sales representatives are referred to instead as vendors. Their interactions with nurses also get redefined so that people don't even think of them as an industry interaction.

I spoke by phone with Mary, the nurse manager for an orthopedic surgery unit at the hospital where Ashley worked, discussing my request to observe nurses' interactions with industry on her unit. Mary asked, "What are you looking at? Like vendors coming to the unit to try and get us to change our brands?" I explained that I was interested in "any and all" industry interactions. She jumped back in, "This really doesn't happen here," citing their policy that prevents sales reps from "just coming onto the units . . . They have to have an appointment, and they have to wear a badge." She continued, emphasizing that "vendors are not even allowed to talk to me . . . The hospital has a committee in which a representative staff nurse participates in purchasing decisions and votes on products presented by vendors." She explained, "If a vendor comes up to talk to me, I send them right back down" to the purchasing department.

During this conversation, I was thinking to myself, How does "having an appointment" translate into "this doesn't happen here"? The policy prevents sales reps from accessing the patient care units—unless they have an ID badge. And sales reps are not allowed to talk to the nurses, but they *do*, and then they get directed to a hospital purchasing committee. What happens then?

I had a number of similar conversations with other nurse managers and directors, who each asserted that nurses didn't really interact with industry, but then pointed out three exceptions: sales visits by appointment, presentations to hospital purchasing committees, and in-service education. I arranged to observe these kinds of interactions, which had been transformed from an industry interaction into something else. In these cases, the formality of the interaction resulted in a blending of marketing with business as usual, but in a way that didn't feel like advertising. Thus, nurses saw the presentation at the committee meeting or in-service, not as a sales spiel, but as legitimate information, endorsed by the hospital.

A Badge of Belonging

Aries is a young, fast-talking, dynamic administrator at a public hospital. I met with him in his cupboard of an office, with windows, in lieu of curtains, papered in children's drawings from the volunteer program for which he is responsible. Still in his twenties, he quickly rose within the hospital administration and was offered responsibility for the Department of Materials Management when its director retired. In this role, he oversaw the hospital's multimillion-dollar budget for equipment and supplies. Describing the department's culture at that time as "old school," Aries explained that "there were a lot of things that were just kind of hinky" in terms of who had the authority to make a formal purchasing request, as well as the lack of transparency throughout the process. Part of the problem, he discovered, was that sales representatives often initiated the requests, using the purchasing committee meetings as a forum for presenting their "newest wares." At other times, they pursued nurses who sat on the committee in their clinical workspaces, "traipsing up and down the hallways." One of Aries's first priorities in revamping the hospital's policies for interacting with sales reps was to ask, "Okay, how do we tie that up a little bit . . . get it a little tighter?"

"What was the concern there?" I asked.

"The concern? Well, it's a lot of things," he explained. "One is patient safety. We should know who's in our building, who's on our units and near patients, in patient areas, whenever they're there. So identifying them," by which he meant the sales reps. "The other piece," he told me, "was just the waste of time—of nursing time and staff time, physicians' time, just like, folks coming up and down trying to sell you something."

As part of the new policy, Aries implemented a system called vendor credentialing, whereby sales representatives registered with the purchasing department and had to check in at an electronic terminal at every visit, obtaining a temporary sticker badge that they had to wear for the duration of their appointment.

Aries was in step with administrators across the hospital sector who are implementing more restrictive mechanisms to ensure that sales reps are identified when they enter hospitals and that they are compliant with the same health, safety, and privacy standards required of hospital employees.[2] All four hospitals I visited had implemented a vendor credentialing system. The Joint Commission on Accreditation of Healthcare Organizations requires that hospitals identify who is entering their facility and why, but leaves it up to hospitals to determine how.[3] For hospitals, vendor credentialing is designed to enhance patient safety and also to reduce hospital liability and achieve regulatory compliance.

A number of companies have popped up to help hospitals meet this requirement. VCS, or Vendor Credentialing Service, now Symplr, is one of a handful of major third-party vendor credentialing companies in the United States. An old promotional video on their website suggests that without the company's credentialing mechanism, a hospital administrator will have great difficulty determining whether sales representatives are safe to be in the hospital and are on legitimate business.[4] The promotional video opens with a narrator posing the question, "Would you like to know for sure that every vendor who walks through your doors is *supposed* to be there?" Text floats behind a parade of smiling red figurines waddling through the hospital doors with question marks covering their bodies: "Hospital vendors . . . Who Belongs? How Can You Tell?" Referencing the figurines with furrowed brows in prison stripes (the "Felon"), in orange ("No Appointment"), and in purple ("TB") that are streaming through the hospital doors, the narrator asserts, "You don't want *this* person wandering around," suggesting that these outsiders inherently pose a high level of security, health, and safety risk to the hospital community, although critics of vendor credentialing have pointed to a double standard, asserting that patients and their visitors may well be unvaccinated felons.[5]

Hospitals rely on credentialing companies to verify a sales representative's background check clearance, vaccination and tuberculosis screening records, and completion of numerous trainings, including privacy and protection from blood-borne pathogens. This service is at little to no cost to the hospital, as credentialing companies typically charge individual sales representatives a fee to register with their systems. Sales reps may then have to register with multiple companies in order to gain access to all hospitals in their sales territory. Certain individuals in the hospital have the authority to register a sales rep in the system and to make an appointment, including physicians, nurse educators, managers, and clinical nurse specialists.

Ashley, as a nurse educator, was one of those people with the authority to register sales reps in the vendor-credentialing system. She would register them and have them sign in to the security system, so that "they're legit to be walking around." When a rep arrives at the hospital at a specified date and time, security will verify the rep's identification and give him or her a temporary sticker badge. This badge signals that the sales rep is present at the request of a colleague on a hospital-sanctioned purpose.

The nurses and hospital administrators I talked to pointed to vendor credentialing as evidence that drop-in sales visits had decreased since its implementation. Sales reps were still present in the hospital on a daily basis, but having an appointment and a badge suggested to staff and patients that the sales rep was present, not for sales purposes, but on hospital business. Thus, these kinds of visits didn't count in their minds as sales calls.

As Aries pointed out, there were two key problems with having sales reps in places where patient care was taking place. The first—maintaining patients' safety and reducing hospital liability—required vetting the sales reps' background and the purpose of their visit. Vendor credentialing was a means of ensuring that sales reps did not have criminal records or infectious diseases, had basic knowledge of hospital safety, and had been invited into the facility. The second and greater problem, though, was how they behaved when in the hospital.

At Ashley's hospital, reps had a history of entering the hospital uninvited and approaching doctors or nurses on the patient care units to present samples or marketing pamphlets or to have conversations about their product. Others had tried to conduct their own surveys of staff to garner information about product usage or seek other feedback. Not only was this a waste of clinicians' time, but such contact could compromise patients' privacy, disrupt patient care, or introduce samples of products that the hospital hadn't evaluated or approved.

In some areas of the hospital, such as the operating room or interventional radiology, the stakes for having reps enter uninvited were much higher than in other clinical areas. These are tightly controlled areas, designed to safeguard patients undergoing surgery from infection and to promote safety and efficiency.

These areas also have high vendor traffic, with sales representatives assisting with clinical procedures every day of the week. Many of these sales reps are given permanent hospital identification, which allows them to bypass the vendor credentialing terminal and check-in processes. Ashley explained the high traffic—a combination of product support during surgeries, product trainings, and informal conversations—as a consequence of the nature of patient care in these areas. The operating room and intensive care units, for example, "have complex patients that require lots of tools or expensive things to make them feel better." Consequently, companies and their reps are motivated to dedicate a great deal of attention to these areas in terms of sales rep presence and product support.

"I feel that, as an educator," Ashley reflected, "my ability to get a vendor to show up is *probably* influenced by how much they think their time here will equal higher sales." Thus, the availability of product support and education was not driven by the complexity of the device or risk of harm, but rather by the sales commission for the rep and the sale of a big-ticket item for the company.

Invariably young and good-looking, suitcase in tow, these reps are at the hospital on a daily basis, know their way around the institution, and are familiar to staff. Yet, they are not granted the same privileges as staff or visitors with a clinical background—for example, medical students. Sales reps in these high-risk areas are frequently required to wear additional identification to make them "stand out" so that they can be monitored. "We'll have a cast of thousands in our rooms," one veteran operating room nurse explained. "You have residents and interns and medical students and observers . . . It gets overwhelming for our nursing staff to know who's who."

Everyone dons hospital-issued scrubs, masks, shoe covers, and surgical caps in the operating room. This standardized costume is the uniform of a highly restricted clinical space, where the only identifying features are the eyes peering over the mask and an ID badge—and once the sterile gowns are donned, even the badges are covered. One of the hospitals I visited had devised a system that enabled sales reps to be instantly identified: vendors were required to wear red bouffant surgical hats. This differentiated them from the visitors, who sported green hats and, although not permitted to engage in patient care, might have access to the medical record; those engaged in caring for the patient, the clinicians, wore blue hats. At other hospitals, vendors were made to don bright red scrubs or surgical hats patterned in pediatric motifs: poodles, palm trees, and monkeys. Because identification mechanisms allowed for instant classification of a person's role, it allowed nurses to monitor behavior. For example, if a sales rep decided to check his or her email on a hospital computer that also provided access to the patient's medical record, the circulating nurse could intervene and prevent a privacy violation.

As a consequence, some of the reps seemed to resist these requirements. Sales reps often stalled in changing into their red scrubs, swapped out the colored hat for a plain one, or changed back into their own set of scrubs as soon as they left the operating room. One sales rep told me about an act of collective resistance in which the operating room staff at another hospital unanimously donned the colored hats intended for reps when the new policy was implemented, so that sales reps remained undifferentiated.

Wearing red scrubs, colored hats, or having a sticker badge enabled nurses to supervise sales reps' compliance with hospital policy. Again, sales reps' presence in the hospital was sanctioned—this time, in the other sense of the word. On the one hand, having a sticker badge or brightly colored scrubs sanctioned the presence of sales reps, granting them permission to enter clinical spaces. On the other, it sanctioned their behavior, granting permission on a conditional basis: sales reps had to comply with the rules. But in either case, for frontline staff, encountering a sales rep with the proper identification suggested that they were in the hospital for a legitimate reason and that they were doing what they were supposed to be doing.

Nurse managers, in particular, were well versed in what sales representatives were supposed to do when they visit the hospital. During a focus group with nurse managers from a handful of different departments at Ashley's hospital, one manager outlined the intent of the hospital's vendor policy: "Any time any vendor is *supposed* to come into the hospital, they're *supposed* to be affiliated with somebody from the hospital . . . So everybody who's *supposed* to come in is *supposed* to have a badge that says who they're *supposed* to come in with, and it's *supposed* to help eliminate the random people coming off the street to pitch their latest device or service or whatever it is." Yet, I sensed that her emphasis on what sales reps were supposed to do suggested that this was not always the case in practice. "They're not supposed to be anywhere in the hospital without our program, which is, they check in through security, get their badge, their paper badge," another manager explained. "But still, somehow or another they still manage to come up here anyway without that process."

Despite the reassurances provided by having a vendor credentialing system in terms of liability, the system often failed frontline staff. The experience of a dual reality—what is supposed to happen versus what did happen—created an underlying exasperation that sales reps "just don't play by the rules." So while nurses could point to the policy and thoroughly describe all that a rep was "supposed to do" when visiting the hospital, there was also full recognition that, as one nurse stated, "they're reps." Reps had a bad habit of "wandering around," "trolling the ICUs or other units," and "traipsing up and down the hallways," trying to gain access to clinicians in order to promote their products by any means. Sales representatives, by design, would attempt to push the boundaries on acceptable behavior.

Many of the nurses I talked to characterized sales reps as nice people. Nurses tend to be empathetic, and many acknowledged the good, hardworking, professional reps they appreciated working with. But they also understood that those working for the medical industry could not act in any other way; sales reps had a duty to their company, which sought to maximize profits for shareholders, not to mention that many worked on commission, and survival in this field required a somewhat cutthroat nature. One nurse manager characterized sales reps as essentially untrustworthy due to the overwhelming financial incentives and pressures inherent in corporate sales. "I don't think they can be trusted, period," he sighed. "You know, that's the sad thing. There's too much money involved."

Although managers and administrators described their policy as effective, the undertone was that reps would seek to bend the rules. The sticker badges gave sales reps a day pass to the hospital. Once their official appointments were finished, they could move freely about the hospital and drop in on whomever, still sporting the badge of belonging. Still, for a sales representative to enter the hospital he or she required an invitation from a clinician; thus it became more important than ever for sales reps to form collegial relationships with gatekeepers and develop a reputation for helping out.

Propping Up a Product

Halfway through my interview with Ashely, she said that she was about to join a hospital committee, "a value analysis committee, which is the group that looks at new stuff and decides whether we want it." She brought this up because, continuing her reflections on influence, "I think it might be a little more intriguing in that group, especially if vendors are presenting." Her other interactions with sales reps all occurred after the hospital had purchased the product. As a committee member, she would be part of the front end of that process. Unlike the pizza lunches for a drug they already used, or the aboveboard, contracted interactions she'd had with the electronic health record vendors, there would now be the possibility of choice for committee members who were tasked with researching and evaluating the available products to meet an identified clinical need. And choice among a number of competing products, for Ashley, created the possibility of marketing influence.

Hospital purchasing committees are known by a number of different names—value analysis, value added, product evaluation—but they share the goal, as Ashley put it, of evaluating "financially as well as medically whether something *cool* is good enough."[6] I attended committee meetings at two different hospitals, but all four of the hospitals I visited had a purchasing committee of this kind. These committees were all chaired or co-chaired by nurses who worked closely with nonclinical people in the hospital supply chain. The committee membership consisted mostly of nurses, including nurse educators, clinical nurse specialists, and nurse managers.

Hospitals purchase tens of millions of dollars in supplies and equipment every year, ranging from "surgical supplies like gauze, Band-Aids, urinals, upwards to, then, capital equipment like ultrasounds, MRI machines, stuff like that," said Aries, describing the scope of his department. All of the hospitals I visited had multiple purchasing committees, including department-specific committees for high-tech areas, like the operating room, or those with unique purchasing needs, like pediatrics (where they need everything in small sizes), plus a hospital-wide committee for products related to nursing care, housekeeping, and food services. These committees generally assessed products that cost less than $10,000 per item, though the total cost by volume per year frequently exceeded this threshold.

When Aries assumed his new role, he was handed responsibility for a $43-million budget and given the mandate, "make sure we don't go over." However, in Aries's view, situating the responsibility —and the control—over a materials budget solely within the supply chain department was both "unfair and inappropriate." First, if a nurse identified a product that she believed would improve the quality of care or the work experience for staff, "it would be unfair "for a materials management person to come and say, 'Well, sorry. That's too expensive.'" Aries explained: "For someone who doesn't have the clinical expertise or clinical background like myself —I didn't go to nursing school, I didn't go to medical school, I've only watched a couple episodes of *House*—it's not appropriate for me to say, 'Well, no, we're not going to take that.' I don't have the background to make that decision." Historically, Aries's department based all purchasing decisions solely on cost, and nursing staff were forced to adapt to whatever product change was the least expensive. But things had shifted, and nurses were now an integral part of the purchasing process. Having a purchasing process that resulted from a strong partnership between nurses and the supply chain was intended to enable purchasing decisions that improved the quality of clinical care and were also cost-effective.

Committees vetted requests from nurses, doctors, and directly from sales representatives, deciding whether to authorize a trial of a new product, which involved selecting a patient care unit to try out product samples and provide an evaluation. In the past, sales reps had introduced samples directly to doctors or nurses, who would begin using them on patients. But when the samples ran out, or a patient was transferred to another unit with the sample device, which was unfamiliar to the receiving staff, chaos ensued. Or, nurses became accustomed to using the samples, just as the sales rep had intended, and it became difficult to remove them, whether or not they were the best product available. The hospital then received a bill for devices or equipment they may not have needed or wanted in the first place.

Aries developed a new policy, whereby the committee would *first* evaluate whether the hospital needed the product and whether it was, among competing products, the best value for money, and *then* allow the company to provide samples. If the nurse heading up the evaluation came back to the committee and reported a success, the committee would recommend the product's purchase, which would be signed off on by the purchasing department. Being the gatekeepers for all new supplies, devices, and equipment, purchasing committee members were thus key targets for sales representatives—and these members were typically nurses.

These committees were designed to act as a funnel for any and all interest in purchasing, to make sure that hospital purchases were based on true need and were given a thorough evaluation. As part of his efforts to better control marketing influence within the hospital, Aries had revamped the purchasing committee process so that committee membership represented a wide variety of areas. Historically, nurses or doctors who were interested in a new product would email Aries, asking to purchase the product. Now, Aries redirected the request to their committee representative, who would put the request to the committee, where the clinical evidence, business case, and operational issues would undergo review.

However, the expectation was that interest in a new product would be sparked outside of this process. It was up to individual doctors or nurses to keep abreast of new developments in their area, or more commonly, to deal with the sales interactions in which reps pitched new products. If interested (or sometimes as a way to get the sales rep out of their office), doctors or nurses would refer the rep and the purchasing request to the committee. What often began as a cold call or a conversation at a trade show was now the first step in a formal process.

There was a tendency for the marketing interaction, which frequently initiated the entire purchasing process, to disappear from view. The sales pitch typically occurred between the sales representative and an individual clinician. However, when the clinician presented a new product request to the committee, or more commonly communicated the request to their committee representative, the initial sales interaction was seldom highlighted. Instead, if purchasing committees sought to vet the impetus for the request, the rationale frequently referenced a clinical need or specialty area of practice that was difficult for fellow committee members, representing other specialty areas, to evaluate. Further, the request was presented through a trusted clinical representative and no longer bore any resemblance to a sales pitch.

Aries continued to struggle with the role that sales tactics played in the purchasing process. He invited me to attend their monthly purchasing committee meeting to observe the process. During the meeting, a nurse from the Interventional Radiology Department presented a new catheter for removing plaque from arteries, requesting permission to try the device in the cardiac catheterization lab. Glossy brochures in hand, the nurse explained that it was not a common procedure and would likely be used only once in a while.

As the only representative from interventional radiology, the other committee members were not in a position to judge the need for this highly specialized device, which would only be used on patients meeting highly specific clinical criteria. However, the meeting chair, Roy, a materials manager who worked in Aries's department, detected an irregularity in the process: typically, devices were first researched and evaluated and *then* a trial would be requested. Roy grimaced in confusion, "This is kind of weird. You want permission to do a trial just in case?"

The nurse, hesitating, admitted that the clinical team had actually already tried the device on a patient. The sales rep in attendance at the procedure had conveniently pulled the device out of his bag and suggested its use to the clinical team. In this case, Roy had stumbled fortuitously upon the true impetus for this product request—a sales rep introducing a new device directly into patient care.

"If it doesn't happen every day, how did they know when you would need it? Are they just milling around the waiting room?" Roy asked, sarcastically.

"You know, they chase ambulances," the nurse replied somewhat darkly, shifting in his chair.

"Did we have to pay for it?!" Roy demanded. "The point of this committee is that we know who and what is in our building," Roy explained, exasperated at again coming up against the long-standing problem of samples introduced by sales reps without first demonstrating clinical need.

The nurse nodded, "It came to $3,000."

"So we just say no!" Roy erupted.

"Then how do I inform the doctors? What if it's the best thing for the patient?," asked the nurse, reluctantly.

"Best for the patient *in their opinion!*" Roy countered, turning to Aries to confirm his sense that the product request had been completely undermined by the dubious marketing practices and backdoor entry of product into the hospital.

"If we trial it and it's worthwhile to you, will it prevent the reps from still milling around? Do we bring the product in?," Aries asked diplomatically.

The nurse explained that given how infrequently the device was required, the procedure being rare, it would be too expensive for the hospital to stock. The practice was to call the sales rep in advance of the scheduled procedure and have them deliver the device and be present for the procedure to answer any device-related questions.

Roy interceded to ask whether there were any competing products on the market, to which the nurse hesitatingly admitted yes.

Intervening before Roy again erupted, Aries said, "In *my* opinion, we need to eliminate the cold-call proposals. The work of this committee is phenomenal, and our next challenge will be to address this situation of equipment brought in for a case with a doctor. How do we get a grip on this?" Seeking to move the agenda along, Aries decided, "We should *not* pay for the trial, and maybe this can be a case study for the group, but we need to recognize that there is competition and leverage this."

"But what if neither vendor will let us trial it for free? Should I send the doctors to you?" the nurse asked Aries.

"I would be happy to have that conversation. We have leverage and we need to use it," Aries said enthusiastically, finally getting to what seemed to be the root of the problem—the pressure from the cardiologists. "I don't want this process to be an obstacle; we don't need to get the cheapest price, but we need a *fair* price. Who is pushing this? I'll talk to them. This group is *not* to be seen as an obstacle."

In closing the issue, however, the committee decided to authorize use of the sample device.

Committee members faced multiple pressures, including aggressive sales tactics from reps, as well as requests from colleagues, some of whom wielded considerable power and influence within the hospital. Aries recognized the need to appear amenable to product requests to encourage clinicians to funnel their requests through the product evaluation process. Otherwise, the cardiologists in this case would circumvent the process and go ahead and use the samples that interested them, leaving the hospital to swallow the costs. Yet, the committee struggled to identify and stem the marketing that created many of the product requests in the first place. In contrast to the convenience of having sales reps deliver samples at the point of care, Aries had to convince clinicians that a transparent, evidence-based, but time-consuming evaluation process would in fact lead to better outcomes.

Sales reps who were regularly in the hospital by appointment often took the opportunity to visit committee members once their appointment had concluded and to furnish them with product samples, which were then distributed among the staff. Retroactively, nurses brought these products to the committee to get approval for their use.

For example, the final agenda item at the purchasing committee meeting was a review of a recent trial of a product designed to assist nurses with intravenous (IV) line starts, presented by a clinical nurse specialist. Speculating as to why the staff nurses had given less feedback than expected, she reminded the committee members of the sales reps and their samples on the units that had turned up long before the committee had reviewed the request.

"Vendors were creeping around this place—remember the helmet guy?" she prompted. "Nurses had trialed it in their brains before the actual trial." Before the committee could approve the use of a particular vein-finder product on a trial basis, sales reps had been such frequent visitors to the units, wearing the helmet and goggle product, that nurses, believing that the product had already been purchased, simply adopted the new vein finder into practice.

Despite formal policies around samples, many nurses described being inundated with branded gifts, samples, and product information. Due to the influx of pens, mugs, chocolates, and drop-in sales reps, the nurses working in case management at one hospital had to post a sign on their door saying "No Vendors Today." Some nurse managers, in an effort not to be rude, dealt with drop-ins by asking sales reps to "leave information," offering that, if interested, they would be in touch. In this way, product samples and information entered the hospital and remained behind when the rep's one-day sticker badge expired.

For busy clinicians, interactions with sales reps were sometimes perceived as a highly convenient source of information about new products, which they otherwise would have needed to research in their time outside of work. Part of the role of a clinical nurse specialist is to identify product failures, to keep up with changing clinical standards, and to research product alternatives—hence their inclusion on the purchasing committee. The wound care nurse specialist had a desk drawer full of samples left by sales reps while in the hospital on other business, which she turned to when faced with a difficult case.

"It seems like it's not very hard to find an alternative," she noted. "The companies are always calling me on a daily basis, and they send me samples on a daily basis . . . so it's kind of easy. I have a lot of products in my drawer." If she liked the sample after trying it, she would call Coloplast or Smith & Nephew or Medline, remarking, "It's not very hard to reach those people."

However, when she found a product that she liked, she presented the product to the committee as filling a clinical need, and the influence of marketing in the form of samples furnished through relationships with sales representatives receded from the purchasing committee's formal purview.

For many, however, the practice of "planting the seed," as one materials manager described it, was highly disruptive. Irrespective of clinical need, when sales reps introduced samples directly into clinical practice there was no opportunity to seek competing products or to compare them in terms of efficacy or cost. Introducing a new product into practice was time-consuming, as hundreds of clinical staff members might require notification and training. If it turned out that a product was not needed or failed to address the identified need because a rigorous evaluation had not been conducted, valuable time and resources had been wasted.

After planting the seed, sales reps attempted to "push the process," deftly facilitating the product's travel through hospital channels behind the scenes. Those efforts started with a sales rep's attempt to find a clinical champion for their product, who would serve, Aries explained, as a credible internal spokesperson. "Realize," he said to me, "that there are vendors coming in, talking directly with nurses, and really using them as their foot in the door . . . The mentality is, "If we can sell this to the nursing staff . . . everything else will just fall into place. They'll do the internal endorsement." If the sales rep tried to push for the product, it came across as a sales pitch. But when the clinical champion presented the product to the committee, the product spoke for itself—neither buoyed by the sales representative nor dressed up in marketing. A transformation occurred; the marketing message was passed from clinician to clinician, and the committee members trusted the claims about the product because they appeared objective when delivered by an expert colleague.

With only ten minutes left in the meeting, I observed one clinical nurse specialist launch into a rapid-fire presentation of a product, saying "I *have* to get this through this month!" Unwrapping a sample skin-prep product for all to see, the nurse admitted that this too had "been snuck in, but there are all the little ol' ladies with skin tears!" She conceded that the new product would entail a cost increase, but she built a case for cost savings by suggesting, "You can use one of these instead of the 4 or 5 quarter-sized adhesive remover wipes, and it is *very* effective." She gave a dramatic and gory example of a patient who had recently experienced a skin tear on his neck, where his central line had been placed, during tape removal. "I am fine to approve a trial, but I want to see what else is out there, especially since I am not sure how this came into the hospital," Roy, the chair, said, noting that the current product was both old and unpopular, but speculating that the request was the result of samples left on the units.

Because this nurse specialized in wounds, the other committee members took for granted her claims that the product was effective; they had little experience to challenge these assertions. Products such as wound dressings or adhesive removers would rarely have high-quality scientific evidence to support their efficacy, none being required by regulators.[7] If a study had been conducted, it was likely to have been funded and conducted by the manufacturer, which is known to bias study results in favor of their product.[8] Rather, the nurses' expertise served as the basis for the product's credibility.[6] Thus, it was essential for sales reps to secure these kinds of clinical champions to guarantee the purchase and success of their product.

Another way that reps could push the process was to assist nurses and doctors in navigating the formal purchasing process. In this way, the sales rep could promote the product through legitimate channels and still allow the clinician to appear as the spokesperson. Busy clinicians relied heavily on sales reps to perform the legwork to get a product through this process. At Aries's hospital, it was accepted practice for the sales rep to fill out the 17-page new product request form he had designed, with the understanding that the rep knew the product best, but also because clinicians realized that sales reps were highly incentivized to put in the effort. Even when clinicians filled out the form themselves, they often had to rely on the sales rep to provide the necessary product information. Once the doctor or nurse signed off on the form, the part the sales rep had played was no longer visible.

In the eyes of committee members, the more the process appeared to be driven by the clinician rather than the sales rep, the more they believed the hospital truly needed the product and that the product was worthwhile. Ashley, preparing for her first committee meeting, was "hopeful that the presenter in the group is the local clinician who's interested in the product, and that's the person arguing for it, as opposed to having the vendor there to prop them up." For her, propping up was "a little suspicious." On the other hand, Ashley found it persuasive "when someone has something they're excited about, if they can explain to me and answer *all* of my concerns and questions about how it works, how it doesn't work, what's wrong, on their own." What was suspicious was when someone "didn't know the ins and outs" of a product; "folks that just have heard about something and think it's really cool," she contrasted. "And then they're like, 'Here, let's have this vendor tell you how great it is. Because I don't actually know it well enough to tell you.'"

The whole idea behind these purchasing committees was to bring together the "many cooks in the kitchen" to make sure that hospitals chose to buy product, instead of "being sold product," as one committee chair put it. Buying product seemed proactive, driven by true need. This is what Ashley thought when a clinician colleague could explain the ins and outs of a product or when the committee received a thoroughly documented new product request completed by the interested surgeon. When nurses presented a new product to the purchasing committee, the claims they made sounded nothing like marketing, particularly when the spokesperson was a trusted, credible, and expert colleague.

The formal purchasing process distanced committee members from the feeling of being sold something. But, as seen with Aries's struggles, the process often only neutralized the *perception* of marketing influence. Sales reps continued to market their products directly to clinicians and had the opportunity to do so because they had been granted appointments, ID badges, or a regular role in supporting clinical functions. Nurses and doctors found these interactions to be a convenient way to learn about and test new products because sales reps reliably produced product samples and information. However, the end result was often the opposite of convenient, when nurses were left to work with products that failed to meet the clinical need after a months-long purchasing and implementation process.

Once a committee authorized the testing of a new product, the sales representative and product samples gained entry into the hospital. If the product was then deemed successful, a purchasing contract was drawn up. Implementation of the new product into patient care required the notification and training of its end users: contracts specified not only volume and price but also the inclusion of company-delivered product education.

Education Supporting Their Product

When I talked to Ashley, she was nearing the end of a two-week period during which the hospital was rolling out a new glucometer, which is a handheld device used to measure blood sugar. During this period, anyone working in the hospital who might use a glucometer needed to be introduced to the new device, including the hospital's 4,000 nurses. Because the high number of trainings would have quickly overwhelmed their education department, Ashley's hospital had contracted the manufacturer to provide the necessary instruction.

A major part of Ashley's role as a nurse educator was working directly with company representatives to develop the script for the in-service and to coordinate the reps' visits to every hospital unit that would get a new glucometer, aiming to reach nurses on both the day and night shifts. When I met with her, she was checking in with the company representatives after two weeks of training. "They're just getting stragglers," she explained, and we discussed whether I could observe. At first Ashley wasn't sure if they'd "be down" with having me shadow, but she also said, "I wouldn't mind them having an observer."

"They're very aware of what they're allowed to do with their materials and what they're not," she explained, referencing the script that she and the company reps had agreed on. In her experience, reps sometimes veered off the agreed-upon content, pitching related products or disparaging competing products. But at this late stage of the rollout, she did not want to jeopardize her relationship with the reps and their willingness to help meet their shared targets by making them feel scrutinized. This rollout had had some "difficulties with the implementation," she mentioned, and had required a "huge collaborative effort."

She reflected that the company reps had gone above and beyond to make the schedule work, "because at the end of the day, you both have the same outcome desired." Like her work with the electronic health record companies, to Ashley, her interactions with these company reps was teamwork. And since she couldn't accomplish the staff training without company support because her department lacked the human resources, she needed to maintain her relationships with these reps.

Although the reps' and Ashley's goals for the glucometer training appeared to be aligned, fundamentally they diverged. Companies offer to provide in-service training and product support as a means to remain competitive and to build a credible brand that suggests shared healthcare values. For example, during a meeting of a purchasing subcommittee tasked with evaluating new gloves, a sales rep, new to his account, assured that committee, "We will do *whatever* it takes, I will be available 24 hours a day, I can do an in-servicing claim at two o'clock in the morning, I will be here all the time, any sizes, samples you need for a trial, whatever." Fulfilling these kinds of support roles however, will only occur insofar as it makes business sense in terms of building client relationships, maintaining a competitive edge, and growing the volume of sales.

Ashley was particularly frustrated at this late stage in the glucometer rollout because she believed the lab department, which had negotiated the training contract, had aimed too low. This was another point at which the company's interests and Ashley's interests as a nurse educator diverged. The company needed to fulfill the contract, whereas Ashley needed to make sure that all nurses were competent and comfortable using the new device. However, the contract specified that the company representatives train 80% of the nursing staff, which they estimated to be 3,000 nurses. "We actually have closer to 4,000, so they're already in trouble," Ashley pointed out. The company, she explained, "is only expected and on point to do 80%. And so they don't have to train the other 20%, which is actually closer to 30%." Thus, ultimately, it was not about the comprehensiveness or quality of the education. Highlighting the absurdity of the arrangement, Ashley went on, "It's a totally different number . . . They know who's competent today, and that number is equal to who's competent tomorrow."

Ashley had also experienced these kinds of in-services from the perspective of a staff nurse. During her time on the transplant unit, she remembered that reps would "come in—they interrupt our day, they teach us something, and then they leave. They take up our time to talk to one another at staff meetings, and they leave. And so as much as we're interested to learn, they're an invasive species, rather than a local species." For the staff nurses I spoke with, the ubiquitous in-service, occurring several times a month, was the primary way they encountered sales representatives. These in-services punctuated a nurse's day, and although nurses emphasized the quick nature of this transmittal of information, they also characterized it as an interruption that they were required to tolerate.

To staff nurses, sales representatives were an invasive species, as Ashley described them, foreign to the patient care environment. A critical care staff nurse described being able to tell instantly whether an in-service was coming her way because the reps stood out, standing in the corridor "in their little outfits with heels, waiting with their little [IV] pole." At the same time, to staff nurses, sales representatives were emissaries from the administration, delivering news that a new product had been purchased. The rep's being there at all signaled that the hospital had evaluated and selected a particular product, and a nurse educator, like Ashley, had signed off on the sales rep's script. Thus, the in-services were judged mostly benign or, at worst, were a nuisance. But for the sales rep, this was an opportunity to meet directly with the staff nurses who would determine whether the product was a success in the hospital and to foster long-term, ongoing relationships in the service of growing the volume of sales.

Sales representatives came to patient care units to perform these roaming in-services after the morning chaos of shift change, breakfast, assessments, personal care, and medication administration, or first thing in the evening after the parallel shift change, and attempted to gather as many nurses as possible in the corridors or the break room to dispense their five-minute bulleted product training. "It's rough," a pediatric staff nurse offered, "I mean you get, like I said, a page. You have to come to the nurses' station or try to if you can, and you try because you know that someone's checking you off and you're going to have to do it eventually, either that day or the next day. And you do want the information, but it's difficult sometimes." This experience was difficult because if a nurse could not attend the in-service due to workload, or if it occurred on her day off, upon coming to work, she might be faced with an IV pump she had never seen before and, as one nurse recalled, "can't even figure out how to turn on," but which she had to operate in order to give her patients' morning medications. In-services were disruptive to nursing care and took nurses away from the bedside, but they were also built into their shifts and necessary for them to do their work.

Ashley introduced me the next morning to Linda, the glucometer company representative, who hadn't minded my following her as she tried to find the remaining nurses yet to receive the training. Her exclusive role was to conduct in-services. She told me about a time she had flagged down a nurse in the intensive care unit to perform her five-minute glucometer in-service. The nurse had asked her to wait until she could grab a free moment, and in the time that Linda waited for her at the nurses' station, the patient the nurse was caring for died. This had greatly impacted Linda and helped her to tailor her trainings to busy nurses. For nurses and sales reps alike, these in-services occurred very much in the thick of it, woven right into the fabric of day-to-day patient care activities.

I also had the opportunity to shadow Dave, a medical-surgical sales rep, who represented a wide range of products. Spearheaded by the infection control nurse, the hospital had recently purchased new medical isolation gowns. When hospitalized patients have an infectious disease, they are isolated in private rooms to prevent the spread of infection, and anyone entering the room dons personal protective equipment, including a gown, gloves, and sometimes a face mask.[9] During one five-minute in-service, Dave, huddled with a group of staff nurses in the corridor of a patient care unit, demonstrated the over-the-head style of gown, the convenient front-facing ties, and the color-coded sizing. Meanwhile, a patient, parked in her wheelchair outside of her room, was retching, and a nurse passed her a kidney-shaped basin in which to vomit while keeping her attention on Dave.

Dave's strategy was often to find his way to the break rooms in the back of units, knowing many of the door security key codes by memory. Despite being employed by a medical device company and having only visitor status, he was at home in these clinical spaces, wearing scrubs on in-service day instead of his typical dress suit to blend in, and possessing staff-only information. Because he was in the hospital often on a daily basis, he was familiar to the staff, and he waved to a known nurse upon entering one unit. Moments later, this nurse proclaimed through an overhead page, "There's a presentation in the break room with *CANDY*!"

The nurses we came upon in the break room seemed accustomed to being barged in on, casually looking up from their bagged lunches and magazines. These break rooms were hardly places of respite, let alone conducive to learning—no windows, fluorescent lights, flyers crammed into every available wall space; mailboxes stuffed with everything from bananas to Tupperware; backpacks and purses stashed in every corner. Dave hardly had space to pull the gown on over his head. The nurses gave up a portion of their break to listen, the time needed for a mandatory in-service taken from their personal time.

While Dave had product-specific knowledge and was a familiar fixture in the hospital, he did not know anything about the context in which these gowns would be used. One of the nurses asked whether everyone who entered an isolation room required a gown or whether it was only necessary for those directly in contact with the patient, giving the example of a physician on rounds accompanied by ten medical student observers. Dave did not know the answer, but rather than admit it, he agreed with the nurse that this could be wasteful. In fact, for certain infectious diseases, not donning the gowns would potentially expose the staff and other patients to illness.[9] Later that day, Dave asked me, knowing I was a nurse, which units I thought might actually use an isolation gown; earlier, he had been rebuffed by the manager at the infusion clinic, an outpatient area where these precautions are not typically required.

Nurses didn't have a choice whether to attend these in-services: for the staff nurses, attendance meant being "checked off" as "competent" on their personnel file, which could then be audited by hospital regulators like The Joint Commission or the Centers for Medicare and Medicaid Services. For the sales representatives, meeting the targets for a percentage of nurses checked off as specified in the purchasing contract was vital.

Dave came armed for a day of in-servicing with a tote bag filled with candy and an armful of isolation gown samples. Traveling unit to unit, Dave would approach the charge nurse, who would assemble any available nurses. After performing his 30-second gown-donning demo, Dave addressed the assembly, "You can have a candy if you sign." The nurses dutifully passed Dave's blank sheet of paper around, collecting signatures and stocking up on fistfuls of mini chocolate bars to last the remainder of their shifts. The signature page served as Dave's evidence for having delivered the in-service, which he would return to the Infection Control nurse who had spearheaded the purchasing of this product and was accountable for training any-one in the hospital who might use it.

The mandatory status of these in-services had nothing to do with the value of the information conveyed. For the most part, in-services were "really quick," as one medical-surgical staff nurse recalled, and "sort of rushed and never really complete; you never really knew how to use the product after the little in-service. It came with ac-tually using it yourself." Nurses lamented the gaps that this form of education left for them to fill in their practice, often learning to use new equipment on the fly or relying on colleagues. One staff nurse referred to industry-delivered in-services as "education supporting the product" rather than education supporting her practice, and questioned whether this really constituted education.

"There's no teach-back method, having the rep ask you to tell them what you just learned, making sure that you're retaining what they teach you," another nurse criticized. "We know the basics, but if something more complicated happens, like, what if a chest tube gets dislodged or comes out, what do you do? Do you clamp? Do you use a hemostat to clamp? Do you put Vaseline gauze? I don't think reps," she paused, "can present clinical scenarios for you so that you know what to do. They're just basically here to tell you how the machine works."

For the directors and other top-level hospital administrators, in-services were one-off, contract-bound events that were simply part of the package of purchasing a new product. For staff nurses, in-services were mostly mundane, a not particularly useful alert from management that a new product was in the stockroom. But for the nurse managers and educators who relied on sales representatives to deliver content that was in line with hospital policy and best practices, and that stayed on topic, in-services cracked open the door to marketing. In-services were opportunities for sales reps to meet directly with staff nurses, to foster ongoing relationships, to inform nurses of different reasons they might use a product, and to upsell related products.

Several nurses struggled with how to prevent product support or in-services from turning into sales speeches. Although nurse educators and managers served as gatekeepers for sales reps delivering in-services, they often did not have the capacity to physically oversee these activities. Sales reps occasionally took advantage of their audience with staff nurses to suggest product improvements, add-ons, or related brands that had not been approved through the purchasing process, and trusted that sparking interest would in this way trickle back up to those who sat on the committee. These gatekeepers worked to "home in on reps, because sometimes they can go off in a different direction: 'We also have this product that your hospital hasn't bought yet, but it really goes nicely with this.' You know, some of that conversation, we limit that down."

One nursing director described learning the hard way that an in-service was not as objective as the contracted script suggested, and reps had used the opportunity to suggest software add-ons that were not included in the base price of the smart intravenous pump purchase. The challenge was that the content that sales reps delivered carried the institutional stamp of approval in the eyes of staff nurses. In this case, nurses learned from the rep that the smart pumps could do all sorts of things, but didn't realize that this was only if the hospital purchased the additional software. Staff came back to the director, saying, "Oh, they said it could do this, it could do that," and had attempted to apply their new knowledge to their clinical practice. In the eyes of staff nurses, "If you brought the person who did the in-service into the hospital, obviously, you trust what they're saying, it's implied." But it left nurse managers in a difficult position because staff began to either distrust the products they worked with, believing there was something better on the market, or began practicing outside of the hospital's policy and procedures.

In-servicing, firstly, allowed sales reps to build a reputation for the product and for the company delivering support, "because they want the product to succeed, and they know that user understanding of how that product works will help that product succeed," explained one of Ashley's nurse educator colleagues. As nurse educators working at a prestigious academic teaching hospital, Ashley and her colleagues typically had good relationships with industry point-people when coordinating product in-services. They understood that a product's success "gives the rep a good name, that they have a good relationship with our hospital, because what ends up happening is sometimes the rep will try to get contracts at other university hospitals." Purchasing committees often requested references from nurses at other hospitals when considering whether to purchase a product. In-servicing allowed direct access to staff nurses and the opportunity to create awareness, and then competent and confident use of a product, bolstering the feeling of being well-supported by that company, which the rep hoped would result in a glowing reference.

Secondly, in-servicing allowed for the cultivation of ongoing relationships with nurses, which completely escaped the view of administrators, occurring as it did beyond the boundaries of the initial purchasing contract. For frontline nurses, the one-off in-service was rarely sufficient to become really comfortable using new equipment, and they needed ongoing product support and troubleshooting, as one might for a new car or computer. A critical care clinical nurse specialist had wanted to introduce proning therapy, in which patients who are on ventilators to help them breathe are turned face down to increase the amount of oxygen in their blood. She persuaded her hospital's purchasing committee to rent a special bed, which rotated mechanically, like a slow-motion carnival ride, to turn these patients face down. Initially, the sales rep provided three classes, each lasting three hours, to 30 nurses working in the hospital's two intensive care units; as a clinical nurse specialist, she was typically responsible for this kind of education.

"So I called the rep probably two weeks ago and said, 'Hey, we could really use another go-round here to try to get as many nurses trained as we can,'" she remembered. Because the hospital did not own, but rented this equipment, "it's not something that I can learn and teach, because they have to actually bring the bed in," she explained.

When a patient was admitted who required this therapy, the nurses would contact the sales rep and the sales rep would deliver the bed to the unit. However, because "it's not something we use every day" and "you might kind of forget," the nurse explained, "when we call them to come, they actually send people in to help get the patient on the bed the first time, and do a re-review of how you use it."

In addition to delivering the bed and assisting the nurses to position the patient on the bed, the sales rep was available 24/7 and was "really, really responsive" if the nurses had any trouble operating the equipment. While this kind of relationship perhaps appeared to be helpful and highly convenient, this was the kind of arrangement that permitted sales reps to be in clinical areas on a regular basis— opportunities they used to approach clinicians to sell their products. Though administrators and hospital policy characterized in-services as formal, contract-bound, one-time interactions, they opened the door to product samples and sales pitches and instigated new product requests that purchasing committees then had to contend with.

From the perspective of industry, it would seem that providing in-services, sometimes over the course of several weeks, during the day, night, and on weekends, was well above and beyond the service expectation outlined in the purchasing contract. Finally, however, in-services allowed reps to influence purchasing volume or to plant the seed for new or related products. Ashley talked about her ongoing relationships with sales reps and explained,

I probably will never get somebody who cold calls—I mean, I would never—I have no reason to entertain somebody that cold calls and says, "Hey, you know, I'd love to come and show your people this thing," because we have all these mechanisms in place. I would, perhaps, entertain the folks that are already here—they're already "in," so to speak, and we're using their products—that have a new or improved way to use something that's already in use.

The purchasing process and the contract specifying the initial education actually served to legitimize the company's presence and purpose over the long term. Nurses' perception was that these reps were formally vetted and were now insiders, a perception bolstered by their frequent encounters with these individuals during the course of in-services and for product support. Sales reps used these opportunities to talk to nurses about the different clinical situations in which the product might effectively be used, thus increasing the probability that a nurse would choose that particular product in the course of patient care.

Because the sales reps' goal is to sell more units to the hospital, they need to convince, support, or otherwise make sure that nurses use their product at a high volume. For example, Ashley characterized the in-service as "getting folks to feel comfortable . . . making sure that we understand how to use things and when to use them." She told me about the recent purchase of a stool-collection system, explaining, "The system's really dope if you use it well," but that "it's really complicated and incredibly expensive. They're like $200 a system. Whereas if you use a nasal trumpet and Foley bag, it's far cheaper, right?"

This gave me a rather graphic image of an ingenious, jury-rigged nursing invention to help bedridden patients with horrible diarrhea. During the initial and then ongoing in-servicing for the fancy stool collection system, the system was not used as much as the rep had hoped. Ashley believed that the motivation behind the offers of additional in-services was "to get us to think it was cool and encourage docs to order it when we had a problem." Because nurses needed to get a physician order to use this particular product, the sales rep had both to be sure that nurses were aware of and comfortable using it and also to plant in nurses' minds the specific patient situations in which the product would be useful, thus triggering a request for an order. However, the device itself was complicated and required added maintenance, and patients tended to resolve their problem quickly. On top of that, Ashley explained, "patients run out of the bed when you try to insert it. It's pretty intense. It's not an easy thing to deal with for anybody involved, even if it is really slick, and when it works, it works incredibly well."

The challenge for the sales rep, she knew, was "to try to up . . . the number that we stock in our hospital. The only way to do that is to get nurses to have to use it and to know how to use it, which none—very few nurses—feel like they know it very well and want to use it." Even if sales reps were able to convince the purchasing committee that a product is valuable, if nurses, who actually pull the products off the shelf to use with patients, don't see its benefit, products will sit around in the stockroom. When the purchasing managers review the order, the number that they stock will either remain the same or even be decreased. On the other hand, if nurses are using a product up faster than it can be restocked, the purchasing department might increase the number in their regular order.

Working under the Radar

As hospitals look to control costs, seeking to do more with less, industry increasingly steps in to fill the gap and, in the process, makes themselves indispensable in the provision of patient care and the functioning of the hospital. On the frontlines of clinical practice, nurses juggle multiple patients, physicians, families, managers, and the real-world constraints of never having enough time or resources. In the middle of this balancing act steps the sales representative, "the perfect friend," who readily offers a helping hand when nurses have no one else to rely upon. From this embedded position, sales reps gain access to informal networks of influence within the institution, forming relationships with institutional insiders—particularly nurses—who effectively run the hospital behind the scenes.

Hospitals have introduced policies to try and control marketing influence. However, by sanctioning the presence of sales reps in clinical spaces, these policies allow for a pervasive commercial presence in clinical practice. While attempting to control costs through outsourcing product support and continuing education to manufacturers, these practices, paradoxically, may increase costs in the long term. Manufacturers will provide these services in an effort to remain competitive, but they will also include the cost of these services in the price of the device or equipment. Formal appointments and in-services create the opportunity for sales reps to interact informally with clinicians, disrupting clinical activities, introducing unapproved samples, and frequently stimulating unnecessary product requests.

This arrangement is a result of misaligned incentives. As long as the people providing product support and education are also working in a sales capacity and, particularly, on commission, these interactions will double as marketing. But ultimately, for-profit companies are not responsible for ensuring the continuing education of clinicians and will only provide these services when it makes business sense to do so. The result is that clinical areas in which more expensive drugs and devices are used are likely to receive greater industry attention, regardless of need. Moreover, education is likely to be in support of products, including increasing diagnosis, treatment, and intervention, rather than on questions of practice, safety, or whether intervention is truly necessary.[10]

Nurses working in hospitals are practicing in environments where the presence of sales reps is normal, and interactions with industry are often built into their job descriptions. This creates the sense that these interactions are benign, and nurses are thus vulnerable to marketing that occurs in the course of these interactions. For some, it also creates a strong sense of ambivalence, a "love-hate" relationship, in which they acknowledge their dependence on industry resources in the service of patient care, but resent the marketing influence these relationships afford these companies.[11] Nurses are increasingly targets for marketing, particularly as policies scrutinize and restrict industry access to physicians,[12] but also because they increasingly fulfill influential roles within the purchasing process and patient care.

chapter 3

"The Perfect Friend"

Building Relationships and Becoming Indispensable

I received a great deal of mail in the weeks leading up to the National Teaching Institute, the annual conference of the American Association of Critical Care Nurses. Every day, I'd empty a small stack of postcards and flyers from my mailbox, each advertising a company that would be attending the Expo at the conference and inviting me to stop by their booth for free Sharpie markers, a squishy eyeball, or a chance to win a Coach purse. And to see their latest products, of course.

One postcard, though, caught my eye: a nurse, wearing colorful purple scrub pants, walks away from the camera, holding the hand of a small boy in pajamas. The boy looks cared for, safe; he and the nurse are walking with purpose toward something. Superimposed on the pair is one word: "Let's". They are going to accomplish something together. Like the nurse to the boy, Hospira reaches out to nurses as a partner, suggesting, as the postcard states, that nurses and Hospira can "Work together," "Envision," "Take action," and "Make the difference." The postcard asserts the power of nurses, telling us, "Everything you do makes a difference." As for Hospira, "everything we do" is to make the work of nurses easier, with drugs and drug delivery systems that streamline nurses' activities and, in doing so, "enhance patient safety." Like a true partner, Hospira emphasizes the reciprocity in their relationship with nurses, saying "We're also here to listen so . . . tell us what you need."

It is difficult to ascertain from the postcard exactly what product or service Hospira is selling, which is actually the point. Instead, the power of nurses, particularly with Hospira at their side, is the focus. The question is why.

Nursing salaries make up one of the largest portions of a hospital budget. Unlike physicians, who can bill insurance for each and every activity, nursing work is typically lumped together—under the charge "room and board."[1] This makes a lot of nursing work invisible, and it also incentivizes hospitals to increase the efficiency of nursing work, or to increase the number of patients assigned to each nurse. Thus, knowledge of nursing workflow enables marketers to frame marketing messages in terms of time savings, efficiency, and waste reduction, like Hospira's claim on the marketing postcard to "streamline" everything a nurse does. Intimate knowledge of these workflow factors enables marketers to demonstrate a product's value to hospital administrators without ever discussing price.

But more than this, partnering with nurses is a form of "synergistic power"—a relationship that feels like a win-win situation in which nurses are enrolled as the instruments of industry promotion but are, in reality, also its targets.[2] Despite enormous budgets and highly coordinated marketing strategies, corporations cannot succeed without the willingness and active participation of those making the decision to prescribe, recommend, or use their products.[2] Marketers must create the sense that the company's goals are aligned with the gatekeepers' goals.[2,3] Thus Hospira's emphasis, for example, on "enhanc[ing] patient safety," a core priority for nurses and hospitals. Companies benefit, in turn, from the legitimacy and trust the public places in those they partner with. Companies like Hospira reach out to nurses so that they can profit from nurses' credibility as members of a profession that is consistently rated the most trusted.[4]

The decision to outsource key clinical functions, such as staff continuing education and product support, to sales representatives is grounded in this sense that hospital and company goals are aligned. Sales representatives have thus been permitted to partner with nurses through a host of formal mechanisms—providing product support in the operating room or working with the nursing education team to provide contracted in-services. This access puts sales reps in a position to influence both clinical decisions at the bedside and purchasing decisions in the boardroom—but it comes with problems. Sales reps are there to increase sales; many work on commission, but even when they don't, they work for companies whose primary aim is to increase value for shareholders. Too frequently, this arrangement doesn't work out in the best interest of patients or of the health system; people may be treated with products that are unsafe or unnecessary, exposing them to the risks of treatments they may not have needed in the first place. Hospitals and insurance, particularly Medicare and Medicaid, then foot the bill for products that are more expensive, though not necessarily more effective.

Why, then, do nurses choose to partner with sales reps?

Sales representatives are trained to expertly employ a host of informal strategies to build relationships with nurses with the goal of becoming legitimate and indispensable members of the healthcare team. This begins with establishing the sense that sales representatives share those values that nurses, as professionals, hold in the highest regard[3]—expertise, lifelong learning, the holistic support of patients. Because these values include providing resources for patient care, eschewing industry support is construed as "denying one's patients."[5] The sense of shared values is bolstered through personal connections, thoughtful gifts, and validation of nurses' expertise. In this way, sales representatives become, as one nurse put it, "the perfect friend."

Though nurses, like their physician colleagues, often developed personal relationships with sales representatives and benefited from the perquisites of these friendships, the "perfect friend" more commonly was the source of instrumental support. More than ever, sales reps have made themselves indispensable in the day-to-day running of a hospital. This kind of friend acts like a team player, is highly responsive to the nurse's needs, and has his back in the chaos of clinical practice.

The nature of this friendship is highly calculated. While sales reps seem to be the perfect friends—paying for lunch, always ready to lend a helping hand—nurses, in their own way, are also the perfect friends for sales reps. Relationships with nurses are highly valuable to reps because nurses are insiders. Under the guise of consulting, education, or informal support, sales representatives can secure allies in promoting their products throughout the hospital.

A Friend by Design

Friendship is carefully fostered with personal connections and the practice of gift-giving. Sales representatives have long been associated with "food, flattery, and friendship," and for decades, have courted physicians in this way.[6-8] A former sales representative described the importance of asking for and remembering key details about a physician's personal life, such as children's birthdays, or scouring the office for knickknacks that would indicate an interest or hobby that could be used to establish a personal connection.[7] This personal connection would later be relied upon in the form of requesting favors—prescriptions to help the rep meet their quotas or impress their manager.[7] Even more important than establishing a personal connection is the importance of exchanging gifts.[6,9,10] According to another former drug rep, these calculated gift exchanges are used to weave the social fabric of reps' relationships with prescribers and are crucial in establishing rapport, forging alliances, acquiring commitments, and eventually, expecting returns.[6]

One nurse manager had worked in the operating room for decades. When he first started the job, he received frequent offers to "fly me here, fly me there, and go to the best restaurants," which he deemed unacceptable, and he set clear limits for the staff and the reps with whom they regularly worked. But he also witnessed firsthand the relationships that developed between nurses and sales reps over long hours standing side by side during surgeries. "The OR is very intense," he explained. "The surgery is long, so the reps are nice guys or nice women . . . and they tend to get on the football teams or softball teams, you know, become good friends with some of the nurses."

First, the sales rep would be invited to the staff Christmas party. Come spring, the sales rep would join the department softball team. In his view, these physicians and nurses were professionals and smart, hardworking people, but they could be naïve about the realities of sales. "It's endless. And it can be very subtle," he emphasized. "You've got a very attractive person, they seem to have a really nice personality, they're taking you out and they're paying for things. The perfect friend."

The person the nurses saw on a daily basis and relied on during intense surgeries was helpful, kind, and fun *by design*. It's not as if a rep turned into a jerk the moment he or she left the hospital; rather, reps are chosen for these personable traits and trained to deploy them in the service of increasing sales.[6]

Another nurse manager recalled a sales rep encouraging nursing staff to give positive feedback on an in-house evaluation of the product he represented. In addition to bringing in a hot lunch or leaving baskets of goodies in the staff room, the rep urged the nurses, "You've got to support this trial because if not, my kids are not going to be able to go to college!" The nurses, whom the manager described as "soft sells," had known the rep for years and capitulated because this particular rep seemed like "part of the family." This manager understood the psychology of friendship and that reps deliberately cultivated favor. The nurses had a tendency to act favorably toward this rep, "whether it's because someone's always been kind to you and takes you out to dinner or buys you cookies or food, or because you develop that relationship." She tried to explain to the staff that they had just spent a million dollars on a contract for new gloves—accepting the sales rep's donuts during the in-service crossed a line. "Next year," she explained, "the hospital may choose to go out to bid again, and if you have developed a relationship with that vendor, because they bring you little sweets and goodies, how objective are you going to be next year when you're asked to look at another product and you don't know that vendor? You don't have that relationship?"

These kinds of friendship were forged over time and often began in the context of working side by side, which the hospital's policies had sanctioned and formalized. The familiarity with a given rep was established gradually and was bolstered through multiple positive working experiences. Thus, even for nurses who recognized that invitations to dinner or even donuts crossed a line, there was openness to gifts that seemed work related.

One clinical nurse specialist had served as a paid speaker for a pharmaceutical company on a Speaker's Bureau about the detection of sepsis, a life-threatening complication of infection, a topic she was highly passionate about, having seen many patients die unncessarily. The company reps offered her all kinds of things, including an honorarium, but she always responded, "I'll take whatever you're giving, but I want it for staff." After one speaking engagement she asked the sales rep to purchase 200 critical care nursing textbooks for staff, which they did. Similarly, a sales rep she currently worked with frequently offered to take the staff nurses to lunch because the unit used so much of the company's product. Recently, there was a quality issue with one of the products, and the reps were grateful that the staff had provided feedback and tolerated the amount of time it took to address the issue rather than switching products. The manager drew the line at lunch, explaining, "people are working here," but instead asked, "Can you send nurses to conference? Can you create a fund for that? When they go to the National Teaching Institute, which is our national meeting, then you can take them out." The reps gladly acquiesced.

Whatever the nature of the gift, however, these exchanges served to sustain relationships and to build social capital, which could be drawn upon in the event of a quality issue, the launch of a new product, or increasing the volume of sales. Perhaps even more insidious, however, were relationships that didn't come with any of the perquisities of friendship. They were instead a highly instrumental form of friendship, in which sales reps became indispensable members of the team.

A Helping Hand

I met with Rachel in the busy cafeteria of the public hospital where she worked. We talked over a steady din of chatter, tray stacking, and clamor from the kitchen. We couldn't meet in her office, Rachel explained, because, although she was thrilled to have had one allocated to her, the only available space was located on a locked psychiatric unit, and it was too much trouble to sign visitors in to get them through security and the double sets of locked doors. I was interested in meeting Rachel because, after a handful of interviews with other nurses at her hospital, her name kept coming up. In the words of her colleagues: "Rachel loves the reps."

Rachel was a wound, ostomy, and continence nurse specialist, which means she held an advanced certification in treating wounds and performing skin care for patients with bladder or bowel continence problems. Her job was to consult on every patient admitted to the hospital with a wound, which included anyone with a burn, pressure ulcer, fragile skin, and everyone who had had surgery. The work load was enormous. On top of this, it was up to Rachel to make sure the hospital stayed up to date on the latest scientific research and products for wound care.

Rachel had an extensive purview. She traveled throughout the entire hospital on a daily basis; patients with wounds cropped up on every unit and across every medical specialty. She was highly respected and the hospital's resident expert in wound care, with an emphasis on "the" resident expert. As she explained, "I get my referrals, usually from physicians. When they accept a new patient to any of the units, they would write an order such as "wound consult," and then they would call me. There's nobody else to call. It's just me. And as well, I do rounds—in the mornings, to just see if any of the patients have been missed." Having in some sense an impossible job, Rachel was both extraordinarily busy and highly influential among her fellow clinicians. She communicated wound and ostomy care plans to staff nurses who cared for the patients directly, and she was responsible for ensuring that all staff nurses were current in their knowledge and training on wound care products and practices.

Rachel had a reputation for loving the reps because she was seen to meet with them often. For her, reps provided a utilitarian form of friendship; interacting with industry was about making her one-woman show possible. Rather than coming across as naïve when it came to sales reps, Rachel understood reps' motivation and so took her own precautions, such as supplementing the research provided her by the rep with her own literature search for other scientific studies about a new product. Yet, unlike nurses who were deeply ambivalent about the trade-off between accepting industry's resources and opening the door to commercial influence,[5] Rachel saw these relationships as an important resource for her practice. Rachel believed that if she didn't meet with sales reps, the hospital would come to a technological standstill, and surgeons would continue to order the archaic "wet-to-dry" dressing that wound care specialists had long ago left behind. Her relationships with sales reps were perfectly functional, she explained, and necessary.

One afternoon, Rachel blew onto a general surgical ward, hoping to finish a couple of consults so she could quickly eat a late lunch. She entered a patient room and glanced at the patient's chart to figure out which of the two beds held the person she was to check in on. After bypassing a blood pressure machine and a visitor's chair and stepping around the first curtain, she greeted the patient. She was there to check on the healing status of the patient's new stoma. When the colon is damaged and part needs removal, surgeons take off the damaged section and divert the healthy colon to an opening in the abdominal wall, which is called a stoma. Patients need a lot of support after the surgery to learn how to manage their bowel movements through this new opening, which empties into an attachable bag.

This patient and his nurses had been having serious problems with leaks, which not only were messy and embarrassing but also put the patient at risk for infection or skin breakdown, if the skin around the colostomy could not be kept clean and dry. Rachel glanced at the bedside table to inventory the patient's colostomy supplies and was perturbed to see a mountain of boxes, rolls of tape, extra gauze, and colostomy bags. Immediately, she knew from the number of boxes that nurses weren't sure which size bag was meant to go with this size of stoma. A mismatch could be the cause of the leaking.

When she finished her rounds on the unit, she stepped into the hallway and called Melanie, a sales rep with whom she had an ongoing relationship and was in regular contact. Rachel had first met

Melanie when Rachel first started her job and wanted to update all of the skin care products the hospital was using. Melanie was incredibly accommodating, Rachel explained, fitting herself into Rachel's workdays. When Rachel wanted some product samples, she'd call Melanie and say, "I do not have much time. Can you drop me this and this and that?" Melanie would promptly and dutifully call Rachel from the lobby, hand over a bag of samples, and leave. Rachel felt as if Melanie respected her time. Melanie's demeanor contrasted with that of other reps, who had hunted her so diligently that if she heard their voice on her voicemail, she would immediately delete the message. Rachel's relationship with Melanie was effortless; it streamlined her work and made her feel supported.

This time, she told Melanie, it was time for another round of in-services. When the hospital had first set up the contract for ostomy supplies with Melanie's company, they had negotiated for a round of five-minute demos to take place over a two-week period, on both the day and night shifts, on every unit that used the supplies—thousands of staff nurses across the three shifts would potentially use the products. But Rachel could see that the five-minute demos, which had taken place months ago, when the products were brand new, had worn off—nurses came and went, and some had missed the demos in the first place—and confusion about sizing and fit was growing. The confusion caused incredible waste when supplies were opened and then discarded, and left patients, already in a difficult position, frustrated and discouraged, sometimes with more problems than they had started with.

This was obviously an undertaking Rachel, the one-woman show, could not do on her own, and yet, it was up to her to see that the staff nurses were up to date. Also, Rachel would not be able to successfully care for the patients if nurses could not fully implement her wound care plans. For Rachel, ongoing relationships with sales reps like Melanie were crucial because the hospital (a publicly funded safety-net hospital) could afford an army of only one wound nurse specialist. Rachel certainly could not train the hospital's thousand plus nurses on a whim. Through Melanie, she ordered another week of company-delivered in-services.

However, Rachel told Melanie, "You're not the one to do the in-services. I need what's-her-name to come," referring to the company's wound, ostomy, and continence nurse specialist on staff. "I need another in-service, and the in-service has to be a combination between having the nurses understand the pathophysiology of why, for instance, the patient would need an ileostomy or a colostomy in the first place, as well as the assessment of the stoma every time they come into the shift, as well as fitting the right bag."

The in-services scheduled, Rachel ducked back into her office to grab a bite of lunch, while sending an email out to the nurse managers to give them a heads-up that the sales reps would be stopping by.

In this situation, Melanie was the "perfect friend": responsive, understanding, and able to deliver. Rachel wished all the nurses had this kind of relationship with the company reps. Rachel was not at the hospital 24/7. If ever she wanted to take a vacation—she liked to visit her overseas family for a month at a time—the nurses needed to have someone other than her to call and say, "I'm missing this bag," or "I have no idea how to use it. I have a problem with this equipment. What should I do?" In this sense, Melanie worked as an extension of herself, an interchangeable part of the clinical team.

Nurses like Rachel are the perfect partners for industry—clinical experts, highly influential, and of the belief that they are able to counter marketing influence. Rachel saw relationships with sales reps as a tool that she could use in the service of her practice. However, the value of the relationship to the sales reps was the regular access that Rachel provided to the hospital, end users, and the hospital-wide purchasing committee. Melanie, for example, was permitted access to the units and got bonus face-to-face time with clinical staff, opening opportunities to bring in her company's latest product or drop off another bag of samples to influential nurses like Rachel.

Although the wound product reps seemed to be indispensable, what the nurses at this hospital really needed was another Rachel, someone to cover her vacations, the after-hours shifts, and a team of nurse educators. But at a resource-strapped hospital, this was not a priority, and so the gaps in practice were patched informally, through Rachel's ongoing relationship with the sales reps. Long after the initial in-services, contracted through the purchasing process, had been conducted, the sales reps could maintain a competitive advantage and guarantee the success of their product by providing a high level of service in the context of personal relationships.

In a highly competitive industry, sales reps have described a growing "service expectation" and the pushing of boundaries around what constitutes appropriate customer service.[11] Sometimes providing help to clinicians in the context of these ongoing relationships exceeded the sales rep's scope; however, denying the request could jeopardize their ability to sell the product or damage the relationship they had so carefully cultivated.[11]

When Danielle's hospital first started using a new device, an implant that helps the failing heart with its pumping work, reps had conducted contracted training workshops for the physicians and nurses. However, the first time Danielle cared for a patient with the device, the rep had stayed with her for the duration of the shift, which was a service that exceeded the training requirements stipulated in the purchasing contract. Because they were a community hospital that didn't specialize in cardiology, and because the device was only used in patients as a last resort, it wasn't something the clinicians worked with regularly, and this additional support was appreciated. When a question came up during this training shift, the rep had called someone at the company, presumably a clinician, who made a recommendation that Danielle needed to pass along to the physician. But her inability to verify the source or quality of the advice, relayed through a rep without medical training, left Danielle deeply skeptical: "It just seems very dangerous that we're trusting people who are not medical people."

The night nurse reported that they'd had some difficulty with the device during the previous shift. She wondered if turning the patient from her back onto her side earlier in the night, something done every two hours to relieve the pressure on her tailbone and heels, had somehow dislodged the device in her heart. This kind of device is not sewn into place, but floats within the ventricle. If it is displaced, not only will the heart not pump effectively, but the device can even damage the heart muscle. After paging the cardiologist, who ordered an ultrasound to determine the device's placement, the nurse had also called the device representative, whose business card was pinned to the patient's medical record. The rep had reassured the nursing staff that she would be available 24 hours a day to answer any questions they might have.

As Danielle was performing her morning assessments, the ultrasound technician as well as the device rep arrived to the patient's room to perform the scan of her heart. As the tech performed the test, the rep watched the monitor, narrating the position of the device to Danielle. Danielle kept anticipating that the cardiologist would stop in any moment to interpret the results of the scan, but the device rep was confident that the device was in place and explained that the physician would await her call before coming in. Danielle thought to herself, "Who decided this [arrangement] was good? This is life and death stuff." In fact, no one "had decided" that this was an appropriate role for the sales rep to fill. Instead, the rep's involvement was a consequence of the relationships she had developed with the cardiologists and nursing staff, who came to rely on the device rep to answer questions, troubleshoot the device, and provide recommendations.

A few months later, Danielle's hospital had to scrutinize this practice of relying on the device reps rather than the cardiologists to interpret tests. In a few cases, the device had caused significant damage to the heart because it had been in the wrong place, and this hadn't been caught right away. They now required the physicians to read every echocardiogram. Yet, Danielle had observed several times that the physicians would call the device rep when they had questions. This particular rep covered a territory the size of half the state, so she routinely gave advice remotely, never having seen the patient. This advice ranged from medication recommendations to patient positioning advice to issues with the device itself. Danielle found it "mind blowing" that someone without medical training could be giving high-stakes medical advice for a patient they had not assessed in person.

Like Rachel and her staff nurses, what Danielle really needed was an expert, trusted clinician whom she could call on at any time of the day or night, someone who had independently learned the ins and outs of these cutting-edge technologies and was also a clinical expert. Unfortunately, these kinds of human resources are not something that hospitals have typically chosen to invest in. I later talked to a cardiologist who worked closely with device sales representatives in the cardiac catheterization labs. He believed they provided an essential service; he estimated it would cost the hospital $1 million a year to provide a similar level of device support, asserting that "nurses cost *so* much in the area!" Getting animated and leaning forward in his chair, he said, "Who will come in the middle of the night to the intensive care unit? Not me!"

The Influence of the "Inside Man"

Friendships often begin with food and flattery and evolve over time when a rep proves to be helpful and supportive. This instrumental kind of friendship is a different kind of seduction from the way the pharmaceutical industry has wooed physicians with trips to Hawaii and large consulting payments, but seduction it is, validating the importance of nurses' work in a way they have long been systematically denied. The consequences of these friendships for patients and the health system become apparent once the benefits are reciprocated. Reps respect and seek out nurses' insider knowledge, then use it to introduce products into hospitals and ensure their success with end users. The influence within clinical practice that these friendships afford reps is insidious, presenting itself as a partnership in the name of patient care. However, for nurses, it creates competing loyalties, which reps use in the pursuit of profit.

While eating my lunch at the Critical Care conference, another attendee asked whether he could share the table. We got to talking, and he introduced himself as Saul, a nurse educator at a prestigious academic teaching hospital on the East Coast. I told him about my research, and he excitedly shared that he also served as a consultant for a pharmaceutical packaging company. At five o'clock, I received a call from Saul, who invited me to join him and the industry representatives he consulted for at dinner. The company was sponsoring the conference, and Saul, a member of the association for the past 26 years, attended every year. This conference served as an annual reunion for them.

I met Saul outside the restaurant, a trendy, high-end Italian affair. We were soon joined by Linda, looking lovely in heels, a cocktail dress, and tasteful jewelry, who gave Saul a big hug and swept us into the restaurant. Linda ushered all straight to the bar, backlit in a glowing orange and suggested martinis all around. She threw her head back, laughing as she and Saul reminisced about the martini-induced fun they'd had last time they were together. Perched on a bar stool next to Saul, Linda asked about the family, filling Saul in on the details of her children's lives.

Midway through the first martini, Linda's boss entered the restaurant, similarly well put together. Julie was the vice president of marketing at Linda's company and had been held up doing an interview for the conference organizers about why her company had chosen to be a title sponsor. She greeted everyone warmly, joking that she had come straight from a flight into a hot cab, throwing on her makeup and outfit in order to be camera ready. Julie and Linda split up in order to give closer attention to their guests.

As the group finished their drinks, they moved to the dinner table, where Julie shifted the conversation to a product they had under development. Her company specialized in pharmaceutical packaging, marketing premixed solutions of drugs used in intensive care to help prevent the deadly errors that can occur when busy nurses or pharmacists mix up the combinations themselves. Over a multicourse meal with wine, they asked Saul about his thoughts on insulin, as the company was currently deciding whether to go to market with a premixed bag of insulin to be given to patients through an IV. This was the substance of the emails Saul and the company's pharmacist had been exchanging. They needed a nurse to walk them through the process: How is insulin dosed? Who brings it to the patient? Would there be any interest in a premix? What are the hospital norms around labeling these IV bags? Saul had helped the company put together a survey to answer some of these questions.

As a consultant for Linda's company, Saul regularly gave this kind of advice. The company had recruited him as a key opinion leader to serve on their roster of experienced and influential clinicians, both to provide feedback and to promote the company's products among their peers. Throughout the year, Saul and Linda would exchange emails, texts, and an occasional phone call, the conference serving as an opportunity to meet face to face. "We find that if we can have lunch with the consultants," Linda explained, "if we can sit down and have coffee with them, maybe have dinner with them, where it's a little more relaxed, we get to exchange some great information and in return provide a nice cup of coffee or some kind of a meal."

Since the 1950s, the pharmaceutical industry has commonly and increasingly used key opinion leaders, rather than advertising, as the more effective way to spread the word about their products.[12] These leaders are paid to speak to other clinicians, to consult, to appear in the media, or to present at major conferences. They usually genuinely believe in the value of the product they speak for, which is why they are so valuable to companies, but they also often overlook how the information they present might favor commercial over patient interests.[12]

Saul fit the bill as an ideal key opinion leader: he worked at a prestigious teaching hospital, was a member of all the key critical care associations and societies, worked closely with medical and nursing students, and was board certified in general critical care, cardiac medicine, cardiac surgery, and neuroscience. Not only was he an expert and an educator, but his connections and his role put him at the hub of a very influential circle. From the company's perspective, this was the true value of cultivating a friendly relationship with Saul.

The hospital where Saul worked, he explained, had no idea he was consulting on the side. Many academic medical centers have disclosure policies on conflicts of interest, which Saul may have been in violation of; however, many do not, and of those that do, most remain highly physician-focused and rely on voluntary disclosure rather than monitoring or enforcement.[13,14] Julie stressed that this kind of work happened on his own time and that there was "no obligation" for Saul to either use their products or to provide feedback, positive or negative. Saul, however, said it was a fine line. Disclosing his activities to his employer would compromise his position, which he described as one of an "inside man":

> I know this system. I know all the pharmacists. I know who is in charge of all of the product . . . I work at the grassroots level with clinical pharmacists, with the person in charge of all the processes regarding the pharmacologic product. And then I technically and systematically introduce this company's product. You have to be able to sell it. You can't just say, "Oh, we need to change everything overnight." They want to see the validity, the rationale—if you are able to [promote the product] without actually saying, "Ok, I'm now representing this company."

As an "inside man," Saul described his approach to introducing the company's product as "bottom up," beginning at the "grassroots" level, on the clinical frontline and within department budgets. He explained that he needed to sell the product in a way that made clinical and fiscal sense to those making these decisions. He also understood that knowledge of his consulting work would color people's perceptions of the product, and that he could not be seen to be selling it. Thus, investing in a friendship with Saul secured the company a loyal ally who could market their products on their behalf and in a way that appeared highly credible.

Saul was an exemplary "inside man." He had wide reach among a variety of clinicians, access to students and recently graduated nurses, and credibility within his institution and professional association. His position within the hospital enabled a two-way flow of information: he could advise the company on how things operated on the inside and what was important to those who might use the product; he could also "technically and systematically" introduce information through diffuse channels, permeating the institution with the product as a trusted insider. Because Saul's colleagues and the hospital administrators had no idea he was paid by the pharmaceutical company, they believed the endorsement was coming from someone knowledgeable and unbiased.

One nurse manager explained that it was exactly because nurses were expert "insiders" that sales reps made the effort to build these personal connections. He described, just as Saul had, how nurses could work the system on behalf of sales reps: "In general, the nurses don't have the power to purchase, but they can help the rep understand the system and who to butter up if necessary or who to watch out for when they're trying to get their product in the facility. It just goes on all the time." Nurses possess an insider's knowledge of the system, including key information embedded within their existing relationships with managers, surgeons, and directors—they know who makes decisions, for example, and have insight into their personality quirks, as well as their interests, priorities, values, and preferences. Accustomed to coordinating multiple interests and the allocation of resources, nurses have intimate experience of these decision-making processes, which they can help sales reps navigate. The personal relationships that industry cultivated with nurses existed outside the purview of the administration or official policies about reps in hospitals. It is this invisibility that makes this kind of influence so effective and so insidious.

Proof of Value: The Human Factors

A few years ago, Julie, the vice president of marketing who had retained Saul as a consultant, was at another trade show at a pharmacy conference. She was working the company's booth in the vast exhibition hall. Looking more like a pop-up fashion store than a booth, it occupied a corner of real estate in the pharmaceutical company row. She watched conference attendees browsing up and down the aisle. Branded pens and other trinkets had fallen out of favor due to the industry's code of conduct stipulation about gifts.[15] Instead, banners offering the chance to win an iPad were visible from down the row. The booth next door had a barista on duty, which created both a consumable gift and a window of time for the reps to chat about their latest products. A line of conference participants waiting for lattes was forming.

Standing at the ready with a handful of decorative lanyards to pass out, Julie was approached by a middle-aged woman who introduced herself as a certified registered nurse anesthetist, a type of advanced-practice nurse. Though the conference was pharmacy-focused, this nurse was attending because she was responsible for prescribing and administering the medications used to put patients to sleep in the operating room. She got to chatting with Julie, being familiar with the premixed packages of IV medications that Julie's company produced.

"Why don't you guys put this on the other side?" the nurse asked, pointing to the large-font medication label that was on only one side of the clear plastic bag of fluids. "Here's the conundrum we're dealing with," the nurse told Julie. She explained that when she walked into the operating room, the patient was frequently hooked up to several different IV lines, leading to several different bags of clear fluid. If the bag happened to twist, she couldn't quickly identify which medication was going into which IV line.

Julie was surprised, but pleased by such candid feedback, and thought to herself, "Maybe we ought to reach out to these people to find out more." When she got back to the office after the conference, she proposed market research in the form of focus groups and surveys, but with nurses.

At the time, Julie's company had positioned itself as an extension of the hospital pharmacy, billing itself as a way to outsource the pharmacy labor required to mix critical drugs that were delivered to the intensive care units, operating rooms, and emergency departments. Julie was beginning to recognize that there were a number of issues the company had failed to consider, such as labeling, packaging, and whether the barcode on the bag matched the hospital's scanner, needed for recording the dose and for billing purposes. When the results of the focus groups and surveys with nurses started coming in, Julie faced a "plethora of information that was around being more efficient when it came to labeling their IV lines," resulting in a complete redesign of their packaging.

These conversations also led to valuable insights about who was making purchasing decisions in a hospital. At first, Julie's company had dealt exclusively with the pharmacy department, which administered the hospital's budget for drugs. But when it came to tubing, syringes, and all the disposable products that come with an IV set, Julie learned that the Medical-Surgical Department made the spending decisions. "And so what's interesting," Julie noted, "is you, as a nurse—you essentially straddle both. Because you have to use both . . . and you give feedback to both of those departments."

Julie adapted her marketing strategy to include the major nursing conferences and got those responsible for key opinion leader development to reach out to nurse leaders like Saul, understanding that she needed to begin cultivating friendships among this influential group. Nurses, Julie explained, "are so key to being able to sit down with and understand, because nurses are the main artery to the patient. They see it all. And I think it's so important for industry to have a relationship with nurses, somehow, someway, have better access to them because I think nurses can drive big, good decisions in product improvements." The entire healthcare industry was under enormous pressure to reduce costs and to do more with less. Pharmaceutical companies like the one where Julie worked needed to find ways to show hospital purchasing committees the value in their products.

A pharmaceutical company has only two options, in Julie's view: claim a breakthrough cure or claim value in other ways. And breakthrough cures are rare. "You're going to have a drug from a company like Gilead . . . that cures Hep C, okay?" Julie explained. "And this isn't, 'They're going to help you live with your chronic disease.' No, you've got these guys, 'No, we're going to cure Hepatitis C.' So it's either going to be big drug discovery moments or it's going to be, 'How do we figure out ways to improve human factors around what you guys do?'"

"Human factors," Julie explained, are "those little things that you spend a lot of time on." Nurses like Saul helped her and her marketing team to understand them: "What's your day look like? How complex is your environment, really? How should this thing emotionally help you feel good about wanting to use it? How does this thing from a human factor standpoint reduce workload? Increase workload? And if it does increase workload, what are all the emotional issues and tangible things like that to get our arms around so that you guys do adopt it?" The nurses they talked to brought them all kinds of feedback, but also requests, which opened the door for the sales representatives to establish instrumental-type friendships like those so valued by Rachel. The nurses wanted small posters they could hang everywhere (bathroom posters were a must) and "train the trainer" packages for busy nurse educators who needed to replicate themselves on each unit by training a staff nurse, who could then pass training materials on to their colleagues. Julie's team quickly responded, taking advantage of the opportunity to appear responsive and to deliver the "goods" that these nurses valued.

What Julie came to understand was that the success of her products depended on whether nurses felt good about using them and about working with her company. She wanted to establish an information exchange—citing both the value in nurses' knowledge and the pleasure of their candid approach to feedback—so that "collaboration" occurred. The result would be to bring the end user something of value, something "that you want to use, that you want to embrace, and it does make you guys more efficient. You do have better patient outcomes." Julie explained that the pharmaceutical industry was at a "crossroads."

> The thing that's frustrating, if I can be candid is . . . I think the end user feels like the industry is pushing their products and services onto them. And that's probably true, okay? . . . I think we're *all* scratching our head going, "Hmm. You guys have got to reduce your pricing or reduce your cost. We've got to come up with more innovative ways to make you guys better at what you do." And that's not cheap, and that's not free. So we have to figure out together, collectively, how to do that well. And to me, that's what's important.

Thus, having an inside man like Saul was essential to Julie's success as a marketer. Without insights from the frontlines, her product would fail. Worst-case scenario, the hospital would receive negative feedback from nurses, and the price of premixed bags of drugs would no longer be justifiable when the pharmacists could do the same work in-house.

Gathering insider insights was, however, not enough. There needed to be an exchange within the context of personal, ongoing relationships so that nurses believed that the company's goals were aligned with their own. An inside man would serve as a true partner, planting the seed throughout his own hospital and his professional networks, suggesting that these products were valuable. Because the value of Julie's products lay in the more subjective "human factors" rather than the hard scientific evidence that might accompany a drug claiming to cure a disease, testimony from a reliable insider and educator like Saul was crucial. Rachel, as *the* resident wound care expert in the hospital, found that when she attended purchasing committee meetings, "They're relying mostly on your expertise, so you don't need to make, like, a *huge* argument. You just have to say, 'Within my experience on a daily basis, I find that these do not work for patients.'" Because interactions between sales reps and nurses like Saul and Rachel occur mostly out of sight, purchasing committees and other decision makers can only take their opinions at face value, especially when they have no idea that the companies whose products are under scrutiny have relationships with the nurses promoting them.

Finding Independence

Burt, on the cusp of retirement, reflected on the beginnings of his career working in the hospital supply chain. In the 1980s, he was working on a loading dock. Come Christmas time, the sales representatives gave him bottles of liquor and big baskets of gifts. "I'm nobody!" Burt exclaimed, "I don't have any say over anything. Can you imagine what the people above me were getting?" There was one sales representative in particular, whom 22-year-old Burt believed was actually his friend. "Now, I didn't do anything to call my job into question. My integrity," he explained. "But, I went to baseball games, the football games. Played golf." Sometime later, the sales rep didn't get a particular segment of business, and all of the friendly overtures promptly stopped. "At that moment," Burt recalled, "Both personally and professionally, I realized: he's not my friend. It finally clicked for me. You wouldn't be my friend if I didn't have that badge on that's giving me my title." After this realization, Burt changed his orientation toward industry representatives: "They're not my friend, they're not my enemy. I have friends. I have dogs. I have a wife. The reps are not my friends." And through the course of his career, he declined gifts, no longer socialized with reps, and prohibited his staff from doing the same, explaining that "there's no reason for the vendor to give you anything. We pay you a salary. You don't work for them."

Because hospitals are increasingly outsourcing clinical and technical expertise to sales representatives, nurses are likely to encounter these individuals on a daily basis and come to know them over time. Though they may be "genuinely friendly, they are not genuine friends,"[7] having been selected, trained, and paid to build these relationships in the service of promoting their products. Nursing education, professional codes of conduct, and hospital policies should be more explicit when it comes to establishing and maintaining boundaries in the context of nurse-industry interactions. This includes rejecting false friendship in the form of gifts, free food, and social activities. It also includes critically questioning why industry provides gifts in the form of conference travel, nursing textbooks, teaching materials, and other resources needed for clinical practice that could be reasonably expected from an employer.

Nurses have unique insights into the realities of patient care and are the primary users of a large variety of medical devices and equipment. Industry rightly values this kind of expertise, and nurse-industry interactions that facilitate nurses' contributions to the design of the products and equipment they use in their practice should probably happen more frequently. But these kinds of relationship need to happen openly, and nurses' independent judgment needs to be preserved. The powerful and subconscious feelings of reciprocity engendered through receiving free food and gifts, whether they are work related or not, threaten this independent judgment.[8] When a nurse is paid by companies for consulting or advising, this poses a conflict of interest, which risks compromising a nurse's clinical or purchasing decision making. At the same time, companies too often glean nurses' expert judgment for free. Nurses should be credited and compensated for their time—but, at minimum, nurses need to disclose any external relationships with medically related companies, particularly when they are involved in purchasing or management.

In the next chapter, I introduce the "as-if" world of nursing practice and address the myth that nurses don't really make decisions in the absence of doctors' orders. Part of the reason that nurses' relationships with industry are so invisible is because these relationships are believed to be benign. If nurses aren't making decisions, how could marketing influence occur? This belief sets the tone for hospital policy, and even national policy, like the Sunshine Act; but the truth is, nurses, as insiders, wield powerful influence over patient care and hospital purchasing.

chapter 4

The "As-If" World of Nursing Practice

Nurses, Marketing, and Making Decisions

"I know that on the oncology unit, because we deal with chemo and different drugs that our patients would get, sometimes we do get drug information from them too," Lorraine, a 30-year veteran oncology nurse, said, reflecting on her contact with industry reps. Lorraine and nine other staff nurses who worked across various units at her hospital had agreed to take part in a focus group to discuss the kinds of interaction they had with industry. We were assembled around a conference-room table, sharing a lunch.

"There are sometimes dinners with the reps that we're invited to, and a lot of times nurses go, because you'll get a couple of education credits, and you'll get a dinner at a nice restaurant. But, I sort of wonder why they invite us, because we're not prescribers, and we don't really have anything to do with what drugs get given. But it's good to get the information, usually."

"That's not true!" a young emergency nurse, Abigail, interjected. "Don't you go to doctors, and you say, 'I want this drug! Give me—— the patient needs——.'"

"Well, not for chemo, you know?" Lorraine interrupted.

"Oh, yeah. I wouldn't know the first thing about that," Abigail conceded, deferring to Lorraine's experience.

I asked Abigail what had made her react to Lorraine's view. Abigail explained, "I'm always recommending, you know? Or just strongly suggesting . . . I think that in some ways, you would kind of indirectly have an influence on what drugs the patient's going to get, or you'll ask your patient, 'Oh, which drug works well for you? Obviously, you've been going through this chemo for a long time.'"

The nurses went back and forth, debating whether they could be influenced by a sales rep. In many such conversations during the course of this study, I came up against the belief that nurses were not important targets for industry marketing because they don't prescribe. When Lorraine raised the question, "Why would industry target nurses?," suggesting that nurses had "nothing to do with what drugs get given," Abigail's knee-jerk reaction was that this did not reflect the reality of her nursing practice; she regularly consulted with prescribers on the appropriate course of therapy. But in attempting to articulate this, she still talked about making suggestions or recommendations or about having influence—words that suggest lesser power and certainly not a final say, unlike the physician order or prescriptive authority.

According to these nurses, the purpose of marketing was to influence an individual clinician's decision making. For Lorraine, her invitation to pharmaceutical company–sponsored dinners, designed to promote the prescription of a new oncology drug, could not be effective marketing because she believed she had no influence over chemotherapy treatment decisions. But for Abigail, treatment decisions were broader than a decision about the initial course of chemotherapy treatment; they included tailoring therapy to an individual patient's response and experiences and managing associated symptoms and side effects, all of which her practice directly addressed.

While exploring the ambiguous scope of their authority, these nurses confronted tacit boundaries, which they reinforced for one another, that circumscribed the way they could talk about—and exercise—the kinds of power available to them. Collectively, the group came up with several examples of ways nurses directly influenced a prescribing decision. Yet many still wondered why nurses would be included in drug dinners, insisting they didn't have any say over prescriptions or purchasing decisions. In trying to reconcile this disconnect, I wondered at the persistence of the well-constructed, institutionally preserved and defended myth that they were "just nurses," who did not make decisions in the absence of "doctor's orders." I call this the "as-if" world of nursing practice—a world that behaves *as-if* nurses do not make decisions.

Nurses, I believe, frequently experience a mismatch between the reality of their daily work and the as-if world in which they practice. When I discussed this experience with my PhD supervisor, Dr. Ruth Malone, a former emergency nurse, she recalled a day in the ER that acutely illustrated this mismatch. On admission orders for a patient with a superficial leg gash and no history of breathing problems, the physician wrote: "Breathe room air." Better than not breathing, certainly, but hardly necessary, except to sustain the vigorous fiction that the nurses otherwise would have been helpless to know what the patient should breathe. Emergency nurses routinely administer oxygen to patients short of breath, prior to the patient even seeing a physician; critical care nurses identify the need for and administer medications, with and without so-called standing orders. Yet the medicolegal community sustains the procedural fantasy that it is only after a physician examines the patient that such treatments (and many others) are initiated.

The fact that nurses have been left out of major policies like the Sunshine Act and that hospital administrators deny any interactions between nurses and industry are further manifestations of the as-if world of nursing practice. Such oversights function to sustain the as-if myth in two ways: it appears *as-if* nurses who do not prescribe do not interact with industry representatives, and *as-if* the potential consequences of marketing influence on nurses' decision making are not of sufficient importance to warrant policy attention.

Even though most of the nurses I spoke with had directly experienced marketing in the form of industry-sponsored dinners and "lunch-and-learns," and had accepted product samples, gifts, or even payments from industry for things like speaking or consulting, many were mystified by the attention of sales representatives. The as-if myth, part of their world since they were nursing students, had primed the way they could talk about their power. Many nurses explained to me that they didn't make decisions about treatments or purchasing, thus, there was nothing for sales reps to influence. The as-if myth is further bolstered by policies, procedures, and hierarchies within the health-care system. The hospitals where nurses worked both constrained their ability to make independent decisions and their access to key resources. In turn, nurses became susceptible to the seductiveness of recognition—the lure of sales reps who treated them as experts or gave them opportunities not typically afforded nurses.

"I Wonder Why They Invite Us"

Cherie had noticed that the better the restaurant, the more nurses were there. This time it was a Brazilian restaurant, a *churrascaria*, where the servers stop by the table to carve off portions from giant spit-roasted slabs of meat. The dinner featured a talk on stroke treat-ment, Cherie remembered, though she couldn't remember which company had sponsored it. The nurses were there: nurse educators, nurse managers, nurses from day shift, pm shift, night shift, float pool nurses. Cherie had worked for ten years at a private commu-nity hospital as a cardiac-stroke staff nurse. The flyer advertising the dinner had caught her eye; the talk sounding interesting, but in the end, she was disappointed by the speaker and the PowerPoint full of graphs, tables with tiny font, and dry research results. "If I hadn't gone to graduate school and taken a research methods class, I would've had no idea what they were talking about." The evening was a nice "night out," but in the end, Cherie explained,

> I would rather go to a talk that pertains to how I can improve patient care. What I can do, if, let's say, I'm looking at someone's heart rhythm and I know it's really high, I would want to be educated. If I'm a new nurse, ok, could it be a pain issue? Could it be that the patient's dehy-drated? Could it be because they're throwing a clot? What's their car-diac output? Those things—I want to have it pertain to what's relevant to me for *my* practice.

The entire experience left Cherie wondering why nurses were included in such events. She figured the pharmaceutical company had money to spend, so perhaps that's why these dinners were so lavish. But including nurses didn't make sense, especially when the content of the presentation didn't address their scope of practice. "If we don't have the persuasiveness [or] power to determine what drugs for the patients to use, I don't see what benefit, why the reps would want to have us go to these talks. I really don't," Cherie wondered. "For example, the stroke talk, I really don't know why. We think of it as a free meal."

In the next breath, however, in response to my question about whether she could provide an example from her practice when she had influenced treatment or given feedback to a physician, Cherie said, "I'll tell the doctor that, 'Hey, I've been with this patient for the past 12 hours yesterday, and I'm having the patient again, and I really think so-and-so medication, or I think not that medication." Reflecting, she thought, "I would say I know more about the patient than what the doctors will know, in terms of the length of time that I spend with a patient." Although Cherie could rapidly draw on examples where she directly recommended a medication or a change to a treatment plan based on her clinical expertise and assessment of a particular patient, she was still puzzled, though appreciative, at her inclusion in such marketing events. Despite having identified her important role in determining a patient's course of treatment, Cherie maintained that without prescriptive authority, she was of little interest to industry.

Apart from the routine in-services and the occasional drug dinners, the only other time Cherie encountered sales reps was at the annual conference she attended. The Expo was an exciting opportunity to see what was out there in terms of technologies new to the market and products used at other hospitals. Cherie was really a window shopper—interested, but noncommittal and not looking for anything in particular. She wasn't there to buy anything, she explained, because as a staff nurse she didn't make purchasing decisions or even have any input into which products the hospital purchased. Sometimes she'd stop to ask a question, and at other times she'd go for the freebies—pens, notepads, magnets, lanyards—and then move on to the next booth. If the product was interesting, she'd stick around to listen to the sales rep's pitch. If Cherie stopped for a minute, the sales rep would scan the barcode on her conference identification badge, which gave the company her hospital's name and her email address.

A few days after returning from the conference, Cherie's nurse educator or manager, both of whom sat on hospital purchasing committees, would get an email from the company: "Cherie, a nurse at your hospital, had questions about Product X," with detailed, glossy product flyers attached. Cherie also sometimes brought back samples of the products that caught her eye—perhaps a new type of catheter or a dressing—and passed these along to her manager. Cherie maintained that she had no influence over the kinds of products and equipment the hospital purchased, and yet her interest in a product served as an "in" for sales reps—she became a conduit for information and samples.

Both this kind of influence and the influence Cherie wielded over the orders a physician wrote on a patient were similar in that they were *invisible*. Cherie's impact on purchasing decisions happened behind the scenes—there was no official record of it. Nurses like Cherie and Lorraine had difficulty reconciling why industry targeted nurses given their apparently diffuse, informal, and lesser powers. They questioned whether it was even possible to influence decision making by influencing nurses, given they did not really make decisions—the as-if myth made nurses' knowledge and ability to control a course of action invisible, even to the nurses themselves. Marketing thus seemed benign, and staff nurses like Cherie felt they could freely collect gifts and samples or attend drug dinners and enjoy a free meal, believing it all to have no real effect.

Tracing the Decision

"I have worked with industry at all levels. Very involved," Vera offered after we sat down in a quiet corner of the intensive care unit where she worked. "It's something that's always been a part of my practice as a CNS." Vera was a CNS—a clinical nurse specialist—who specialized in adult critical care. The ICU was her home base, but she would be called to consult on critical care patients anywhere in the hospital. Vera had counterparts in the Emergency Department and on the cardiovascular unit, and these clinical nurse specialists served as linchpins, working with the nursing staff, unit managers, administrators, physicians, and with interdisciplinary services like physical therapy and respiratory. These masters-prepared nurse specialists reviewed the hospital's policies and standards of care to reflect the latest scientific evidence, but rather than slapping a re-search article down at the bedside for nurses to read, they led the implementation of new technologies and processes to ensure a smooth and comprehensive transition. Part of being up to date was keeping abreast of the latest devices, equipment, medications, and supplies, which frequently brought specialists like Vera into contact with sales reps.

"I manage one thing in particular—our Continuous Renal Re-placement Therapy Program," Vera said, pointing to a room down the hall, "A patient was on it over there." Patients in the ICU who have kidney failure might be prescribed this form of continuous di-alysis, in which their blood is filtered through a catheter and is then purified by an attached pump, performing the work of the kidneys until they can heal. Vera had recently seen an integrated pump at a conference and had stopped and checked it out, noting that it was better than what they used at her hospital—previously the best on the market—but with its own safety issues. She arranged for the company to come for a meeting with the hospital's biomedical en-gineers. Sitting around the table, Vera, the nurse managers, and the engineers discussed, "Is this something we want to try here, and coordinate a trial using it on patients?" In the end, they decided to shop around and opted to bring in a second pump made by another company and compare the two side by side. The staff nurses and managers tested out the pumps, as did the engineers and the phy-sician specialists, but in the end, Vera reflected, "I'm the one that really will make [the decision]—I mean, I work with the docs, and if they said, 'Well, we really like this one, but we know nurses are doing the therapy. We order it, but you guys are doing it. You need to tell us what works for you.'"

Vera didn't make purchasing decisions—that was the purview of the manager in the purchasing department. Neither did she order continuous dialysis therapy for patients in kidney failure. But she was certainly pulled into the purchasing process when a clinical evaluation was necessary for new equipment. And in the case of these big-ticket items, like continuous dialysis machines, she had enormous influence. By researching machines on the market, selecting which machine to trial, leading the in-house evaluation, and making the final recommendation, Vera's decisions were foundational to the final purchasing order. And once the machine had been acquired, Vera was responsible for seeing that the staff nurses could operate it safely and competently, contributing to the success of this therapy in the care of patients with kidney disease.

Nonetheless, even Vera, who wielded this degree of influence, could point to why it was so difficult to trace the influence of marketing targeted at nurses on critical purchasing and treatment decisions. "It gets lost in the 'I didn't buy this, I'm not ordering this drug. I'm not even ordering this therapy,'" she explained. "So, it gets lost in, 'Well, how are you this remote kind of nurse?' 'Well, I was leading the clinical evaluation, but I don't prescribe the therapy.'" As she reflected, "There's no direct link back to me in terms of, 'I got this device in here, and all their fluids,' and it's a big business for that company, but I don't control the purchasing volume, whereas physicians and providers *do,* and so there's a direct link there. But if you looked at how much we've paid for different therapies or devices or *supplies,* that's a big chunk of change." Unlike physicians' prescribing, Vera's highly influential decision making was invisible, happening behind the scenes; she characterized her influence over institutional decisions as "remote." Yet, the end results of her influence added up. These machines were a significant investment for the hospital in terms of upkeep and staff training.

This invisibility perhaps partially explains why no one has taken up the issue of nurses' interactions with industry and how they might influence patient care: the influence of marketing on nurses' decisions is very difficult to measure. Researchers have been able to study how marketing influences doctors' decisions because the number and cost of prescriptions is tracked and attributed to individual prescribers. Because doctors in the United States are covered under the Sunshine Act, the number, type, and amount of payments individual doctors receive from industry is also now recorded, enabling associations between marketing and prescribing outcomes to be calculated.[1-3]

The as-if myths around nursing practice are also at work. Some months ago, Vera received an email from the chief nursing officer, copied to a number of other directors, nurse managers, and clinical nurse specialists. The email read, "Somebody wants to do a study about industry and wants access to the hospital, what do you think?" One of the directors hit reply all, dismissing the idea, "Oh, the nurses don't have much interface with them." Vera exploded at her computer and may even have responded, "Are you freaking kidding me?" or words to that effect. She said, "They are so disconnected, our administrators," thinking of twenty examples of recent interactions she'd had with industry.

The email exchange made Vera wonder, "That's maybe *why* there aren't policies. Maybe there's a knowledge gap—if they don't know what's going on, why would they address it?" Vera's thoughts highlighted how the as-if myth allows hospitals to run under the assumption that nurses do not interact with industry and therefore operate "as-if" marketing does not occur.

"If I worked in a place where they said, 'You can't have industry contact—it all goes through someone else,' that to me would be stunting progress," Vera said. "But there are clear boundaries that need to be maintained that we don't talk about enough in nursing. Because the influence is there, and I've seen it, and I'm always in check with myself about that, as I am with all professional boundaries."

The "As-If" World of Nursing Practice

In the "as-if" world, nurses used a particular language to describe their role in treatment and purchasing; instead of talking about decisions they made, nurses frequently used the word *influence*. A major theme at the National Teaching Institute the year I attended, hosted by the American Association of Critical Care Nurses (AACN), was nurses' capacity to "influence." As I flipped through the program, I noticed that the conference featured several sessions about influence, including a two-day leadership seminar, jointly presented by the AACN and VitalSmarts, a consulting company that advertises itself as an "innovator in corporate training and organizational performance." The seminar was billed as providing "the ideal combination of strategies and skills designed to help create profound and sustainable positive changes and influence—with or without formal authority," which implicitly acknowledged that many of the conference attendees were not formal "decision makers." Promoting skill sets for those "with or without formal authority" both reinforced the as-if myth that nurses do not have decision-making capacity and also undermined it by suggesting that nurses had the power to create change.

The Expo opened on the second day of the conference, and I stood in a line hundreds of nurses long, waiting for the doors to open. The booths I had pictured were actually floor displays, some measuring close to 500 square feet. Within these booth spaces, the big companies—GE Healthcare, Baxter, Stryker, Hospira—had display areas, with sales reps at the ready, coffee stations, cake-cutting tables, photo booths, and mini classrooms. The ExpoEd program, which came in the tote we all received at registration, detailed the 25-minute sessions that ran continuously in these classrooms. Industry echoed the official conference theme of "influence" during the trade show: GE Healthcare was scheduled to host the session, "Personal Influence in Pursuit of Excellence."

I approached the GE Healthcare booth just before the session, sliding into a row in the mini classroom, where 30 or more people were already assembled. Gardens of fake flowers ringed the floor display, offsetting the bright lights. A sales rep with a voice fit for radio introduced the speaker, Marilyn, a nurse leader and a paid speaker for GE Healthcare. During the session, Marilyn defined *influence* as producing effects on the actions of others. She explained that influence happened at three levels: the personal, the social, and the structural. She suggested that nurses focus on the personal and the social, giving examples like bringing in a chair-massage therapist, running workshops on giving feedback as a skill set, or "effective communication," noting that if you can "effectively communicate the importance of your idea, you can make a case to raise it on the budget as a priority." She acknowledged that the structural—things like budgets, policy, hierarchies, physician relations—was "tricky" and "full of rewards and punishments," brushing it aside as a concern for nursing influence.

Marilyn, in cautioning nurses against taking on formal structures and power relations, reinforced the idea that nurses' power was most effectively asserted informally and at the individual level. Yet, she also pointed directly to the fact that nurses do have influence and that it can be used to affect budgets and priorities—something of great interest to companies like GE Healthcare.

This is the reality of the as-if world in which nurses work. The "structural" level the GE speaker referred to created conditions that frequently checked nurses' ability to effect change. These constraints also limited nurses' ability to make decisions concerning the delivery of patient care and inhibited their control over the resources needed to perform that care.

Creative Resistance: The Role of Work-Arounds

Michelle was a clinical nurse specialist who worked on a medical intensive care unit. Late one morning, a staff nurse approached Michelle to consult on a newly admitted patient. The staff nurse had conducted her initial assessment and determined that the patient was at high risk for developing pressure ulcers. This patient would be confined to bed for long periods, and had arrived sedated and connected to a mechanical ventilator, unable to roll over or turn in bed by herself. Lying for hours on bony areas like heels, hip bones, or tail bones causes the skin to break down and form an ulcer, which is painful and difficult to heal. In addition to implementing a regular protocol for turning the patient and keeping her well-hydrated and her skin clean and dry, the staff nurse assessed her to be an excellent candidate for a specialty bed. The unit had a number of specialty beds, with air mattresses that could help to relieve the pressure and prevent skin breakdown. Michelle agreed this would be an appropriate intervention. The trouble was, they needed a physician's order to begin using the bed. Michelle paged the physician, but she and the residents had already been by on morning rounds by the time the patient was admitted. There was a chance someone would pop by later that afternoon to write the order, but other priorities were likely to intervene. In the meantime, pressure ulcers only took a matter of hours to begin to form.

The next day, Michelle pulled the attending physician aside and explained the dilemma. It was the nurses who did the pressure ulcer risk assessment, monitored for signs of skin breakdown, instituted a host of other preventive measures, and cared for wounds, should they form. Having to chase down an order for a specialty bed meant delaying care that both the physician and nurses knew to be appropriate and effective. Together, they devised a work-around. The physician would write a standing order for every patient admitted to the ICU for a specialty bed. That way, the nurses could implement the order on the basis of the assessments they were performing anyway.

Michelle articulated her frustration with these kinds of obstacle. In so many areas of critical care practice—patient monitoring, wound care, prevention of patient deterioration—she explained, nurses conducted the assessments, made treatment decisions, implemented therapies, and evaluated their outcomes. "I think there's a lot that nurses have within their scope, according to the Board of Registered Nursing," she reflected, "but it can get complicated by whether or not we need a doctor's order when a patient is in a specific institution." Institutions typically require a doctor's order for billing purposes, which also serves as a cost-control measure. The order allows hospitals to keep track of patient care interventions that can be submitted for reimbursement. The work-around in the case of the specialty bed—writing orders on every patient—allowed nurses to execute the order at their discretion, though doing so under the guise of the physician's "decision." This meant that Michelle could circumvent a structural constraint, but it also meant the as-if myth was maintained; the decisions the nurses had made leading up to these blanket orders remained invisible.

Michelle did a great deal of work around electronic patient monitoring, a fast-growing and highly lucrative sector of the healthcare business, which includes hardware and software that continuously monitors a patient's vital signs—heart rate, respiration rate, blood oxygen level—integrates this data with the patient's electronic health record, and provides data analytics. The Joint Commission, which accredits hospitals in the United States, also releases National Patient Safety Goals, which identify the highest priority patient safety issues and outline performance targets for each goal that hospitals must meet.[4] One of these goals is to "reduce the harm associated with clinical alarm systems."[4] Michelle was a member of the hospital's alarm management task force, which was responsible for addressing this safety issue and meeting the Joint Commission's standards.

The hospital had first purchased electronic vital-signs monitors from Philips for the intensive care unit and the emergency room, but had recently rolled them out to the medical-surgical units with patients who were much less sick. This left the hospital with different versions and models of the equipment, including multiple generations of the same software and hardware. Michelle thought, "Some of that variation is probably appropriate, given the different patient populations, but really, *is* it appropriate?" Each machine came programmed with its own set of defaults; for example, it would set off an alarm to alert the nurse if the patient's heart rate or blood oxygen level had exceeded the default parameters. The task force, Michelle explained, needed to figure out, "What *are* the different defaults? What are the different types of alarms that are happening, and are those alarms meaningful alarms, or are they nuisance alarms?" Nuisance alarms were a major safety issue—staff quickly became desensitized to alarm signals, and the resulting noise and flashing alerts when they went off, because the patient often turned out to be fine. Over time, staff would tune out or even disable alarms, which could result in missing an alarm when it really mattered.

As it turned out, these machines collected an enormous amount of data about each patient, data that could be used to answer these questions. The Philips system exported this data and dumped it onto a server, but Michelle explained that the hospital didn't have the resources to deal with it: "We can't just necessarily hire some full-time people to do data analysis for us based on all this rich data that we have, and so we're partnering with the vendor."

The task force first tried to engage a scientist who worked for Philips to do the data analysis, but the relationships got tangled up with the hospital lawyers and the contractual agreements they would need. Interestingly, however, as Michelle explained, "there are some other clinicians within Philips who do site assessments for different hospitals. They come in to look at default parameters in specific units, kind of take a snapshot look at the different types of alarms that are happening in that environment so that we can compare." The clinical team from Philips had actually come to the hospital, and with Michelle and other members of the alarm task force had done a walk-through of all the units where their monitors were in use. They were currently preparing a report for the task force. Michelle was in the process of working with the administration to facilitate a return visit from the Philips team to continue these evaluations and to answer the questions the task force had raised.

"But the challenge," Michelle explained wryly, "is that *that* work —them looking at the different units and looking at similarities and variations—is a way that Philips can figure out what we might need to upgrade when it comes to our equipment or it comes to our software packages."

"You always have to keep in mind, I think, What's in it for *everyone* involved?," Michelle cautioned. Despite what Philips's motivations in offering help were, Michelle believed the insights that would come out of the report could benefit patients, their families, and overall safety. She understood that it was a balance; in her eyes, both the hospital and Philips were business entities with their own interests, and she attempted to navigate between these interests for the benefit of patients.

For Michelle, working with Philips was a work-around to the hospital's unwillingness or inability to hire someone to analyse their patient data, analysis needed to drive evidence-based changes in setting safe and effective alarm parameters. "What we need the most right now is to decrease the number of these nuisance alarms that are happening," she explained, "and if we're going to do that effectively, we need to get people on a consistent page as far as default settings."

It drove Michelle crazy that nurses had to rely on what the physician had ordered as far as the default parameters for a patient's vital signs, such as heart rate, respiration rate, or blood oxygen level, while knowing "full well that those parameters may not fit this particular patient, and that customization needs to happen." Patient monitoring, Michelle asserted, should be a nurse-driven process. However, she hadn't made any headway with the administration on her own in changing these practices. She decided that she needed to go to the administration with data and insights derived from looking at all the alarms over time. Without the Philips team, there was no way she could collect the evidence she needed to advocate for the changes nurses needed on the front line.

For Michelle, interacting with industry was a work-around to structural constraints, such as nurses having to rely on physician orders for activities over which they had full purview. She asserted that nurses could directly interact with the companies who made the products. "The relationship between industry and the nurses could be a lot more straightforward if the nurses could more outwardly express the things that they need at the bedside and the things that really should be within their control. Then the vendors would be tasked with responding to that." For her, industry representatives were responsive, attuned to her needs, and could address clinical problems through better product design. A patient safety issue like alarm fatigue is complex and has multiple causes, and Michelle thought that working with industry on product solutions was the most straightforward way to address the problem, much more so than tackling the "tricky" structural concerns referenced by the paid speaker from GE Healthcare, such as adjusting the scope of nursing practice, working with physicians, or addressing staff shortages and burnout.

A hallmark of nursing practice is developing "work-arounds" to structural obstacles—from jury-rigging equipment to using physician orders strategically—essentially, working *around* authority. However, a work-around, by definition, often leaves a root cause untouched, allowing it to appear as-if it didn't exist; in this case, better product design might solve problems related to alarm fatigue but not to the nurses' lack autonomy over their own practice.

Work-arounds are prompted by being cut off from the knowledge, resources, or authority needed to act; by nature, they are indirect and require the cobbling together of various actors and resources that are not intended to go together: a latex glove twisted around a syringe delivering chemotherapy to protect the administering nurse from exposure; the "third hand" borrowed from a colleague to operate a blood collection system; the use of multiple underpads to reinforce a defective product, prone to tearing. Work-arounds create solutions for gaps that are not supposed to exist, and because they are indirect and are enacted between and around formal structures and processes, they tend to be invisible. Work-arounds are seldom officially sanctioned and are generally treated with a measure of "see no evil, hear no evil, speak no evil," so institutions can operate as-if work-arounds neither occurred nor were required in the first place. They also serve to hide the ways in which power relations are reproduced and resources really allocated.

In some ways, they are a quintessential example of nursing practice, which struggles against invisibility in an economic and political climate that treats nursing labor as a cost rather than an asset because hospitals cannot bill for nurses' work beyond "room and board."[5,6] Work-arounds are a different kind of power, a form of creative resistance that looks very different from that deployed by formal hospital decision makers; the work of the work-around goes largely unrecognized and thus is given little value. It is a form of action that serves to bolster the as-if myth by obscuring nurses' autonomous actions.

The resulting environment can create relationships of dependence. Just as Michelle and her team turned to Philips to help address their patient safety goals, industry sometimes becomes central to the creation of work-arounds, for example, when nurses find themselves sidelined by formal structures and lacking access to knowledge or resources they need. Anne, the nurse manager of a kidney dialysis unit, had a new project recently dumped in her lap. The hospital was opening a new outpatient dialysis center and was about to purchase a new set of apheresis machines, used to separate blood cells during dialysis, a process that cleans the blood in place of the kidneys. The machines on Anne's inpatient unit would soon be obsolete, and the hospital wanted to replace them at the same time they bought the machines for the new center—that way they could buy them in bulk to drive down the price.

Anne had a number of other work-related priorities, but this was driven by "other people's timelines" and was shaping up to be a "big pain in the neck." The dialysis unit was rather siloed from the rest of the hospital due to the high degree of specialization in technology and therapy. Although there were formal purchasing pathways in place, the process of acquiring specialty equipment didn't always fit, given that this specialty was something of a clinical outlier. Thus, while it appeared as-if there were policies and procedures in place that followed a typical chain of command, in reality, Anne was left to fill the gaps in the process and was the informal (and unrecognized) purchasing authority. Anne was the only nurse manager in dialysis at the hospital, so it was up to her and her alone to figure out which machine to purchase, how to bring it in and to see that all the nurses were trained on its use once it was rolled out to the units. She described the process as "a nightmare."

"Just to get the contract, get the supplies, get the trainer, get people trained, validate that this machine is at least as effective as our old machine," Anne recounted. "It's just very time-consuming, and there's really no support to do that. It kind of falls to me." Anne had reached out to the Lab Department to see if they had a plan for validating the new machines but was told that it was her responsibility. Then she reached out to the Materials Department to see if they had drawn up a purchasing contract, but because the equipment was so specialized and only for her unit, they bounced it back to her. Trying to figure out what to do with the old machines, she reached out to Environmental Services and was told that she had to order their disposal.

In the end, Anne found a work-around: "The vendor is probably more helpful than anybody else at the medical center in getting the things in place." She explained, "I don't necessarily think it should be me having that interaction, but it is by default . . . You have to kind of be the go-between." The sales rep was the only other person who was both motivated and equipped to help Anne bring in the new machines. The sales rep was readily prepared to provide support for product research, contract writing, staff training, and regulatory information, offering Anne a mechanism to work around the obstacles created by the bureaucracy and providing her access to specialized skills and knowledge. In Anne's view, the sales rep was not only an effective work-around, but more reliable and more empowering to Anne than members of her own institution.

In serving as a work-around, the sales rep fixed a problem that wasn't supposed to exist; the hospital administration didn't intentionally isolate Anne or prefer that she work outside of the existing systems. The way the system was structured allowed it to appear as-if Anne wasn't making these decisions independently, and certainly as-if the sales representative had no influence over the process. But the truth was, Anne was cut off from the expertise and support she needed to get the job done. The sales rep provided a solution that bridged this gap, allowing Anne to move on to her patient-related priorities. Using the sales rep as a work-around, however, did nothing to address Anne's not having the institutional support she needed. The sales rep was able to carve out a niche for his or her company by developing this special relationship with Anne, one on which she was dependent. But having this kind of dependent relationship meant Anne could be vulnerable to marketing—without a second set of eyes or outside opinions, Anne could only rely on the information the sales rep delivered, which was certain to be skewed in favor of the company's product.

"It Gives Me a Voice"

Work-arounds and the wider "as-if" culture that nurses worked within had the secondary effect of erasing the decisions nurses made and making much of the work nurses do invisible. On one hand, believing there was no room for industry influence in the absence of formal decision-making powers, nurses regarded marketing as benign. But it also opened a window for industry representatives: providing nurses with recognition.

The experience of being treated by industry as respected, knowledgeable professionals contrasted with nurses' day-to-day experiences, where they regularly had to devise clever work-arounds to surmount medicolegal and bureaucratic obstacles that preserved physician authority and bureaucratic surveillance. Marketers were clearly cognizant of these power dynamics within healthcare. As I wandered around the critical care conference Expo, I was bombarded with messages that would be out of place—and considered to be greatly overstepping one's "place"—were they directed at physicians: for example, the leaflets proclaiming Dräger's mission, "Empowering Heroes to Heal," and the chance to pose for a photo with a male model dressed as superman under a comic book-themed banner, "Nurses are superheroes!" Or Baxter's booth, complete with an espresso station where nurses could collect a free coffee under a banner proclaiming, "For providing care and comfort to those most critical, we thank you," complete with a backdrop of a thoughtful nurse posing beside the words, "I am a thinker, practitioner, researcher. I'm a body of incredible knowledge and unimaginable experiences. I want to be part of building a better way forward." Messages like this tap into the realities of the as-if world of nursing practice, where nurses are frequently disempowered, unrecognized, and lack control over resources needed to affect their practices. The as-if myth also makes nurses susceptible to marketing that offers access to resources and recognition denied by colleagues, physicians, or administrators.

The Expo was about more than just free coffee. Marketing spaces were one of the few places where nurses' power and the value of their work were explicitly recognized; industry gave nurses the sense that their knowledge, judgment, and practices mattered, elevating their perceived status as clinicians, especially compared with physician colleagues.

Morgaine, an ICU staff nurse, described ICU culture as different from what nurses on the units experience in terms of their relationships with physicians. "I've been there a long time and some of those doctors have been there a long time," she reflected. "So it's very collegial, and there's also a lot we've done together socially even." When a drug dinner targeted to the ICU was advertised on a flyer in her unit's breakroom, it included both the physician specialists and the nurses.

"It was kind of like a date, a little girlfriend date, and so we met some other friends there and at each table—there are probably 8 tables, each seating about 10 people—so it's not a small group," she recalled of the last dinner she'd attended. "It's mostly the cardiologists who were there, I think—well, whatever the drug was," she tried to remember. "The intensivists were there and probably some of the neurosurgeons were there." The experience was very social, with "the mixed group of doctors and nurses, and there's wine being poured, which people are drinking, and first the salad will be served and you have the bread."

Including nurses at a pharmaceutical industry-sponsored dinner, alongside their physician colleagues, implied that nurses were equal and crucial members of the clinical team. After the main course had been served, the presenter started the PowerPoint with a brief disclaimer about the sponsorship. People relaxed with their glass of wine, and Morgaine explained, "Anyone could ask a question. So I didn't feel there was a bias, even though the doctor would be the ordering party, and [the one] who would ultimately really make the decision about what they wanted for their patient."

"The presenters were very open to questions from doctors *and* nurses," Morgaine asserted. "Because they understand that we're the ones actually at the bedside administering the drug . . . they know that the nurses are the ones at the bedside titrating it and administering it." For Morgaine, it was clear why the drug company included nurses in these events, and it validated her practice to be given the same consideration as the specialists. "They want to definitely have your buy-in because you're going to be advocating for that." Morgaine explained that ICU nurses often worked from protocols that had broad parameters within which the nurses would choose the most appropriate therapy. "And obviously, you're going to talk to the doctor, but if they're not there, you're just going to make your own decision based on what your order set is. So, they want you to choose that drug too." The drug dinner, Morgaine related, was focused on the care of the person in the ICU. "They understand the nurses, that the intensity of the care is as it is and that you're the one who's constantly there at the bedside, so they want your buy-in," she explained. For nurses who often had to reconcile a discourse of constrained influence with the realities of their skilled, knowledge-able, and discretionary practice, this experience was refreshing.

However, there was a risk that nurses' attention and influence could be had cheaply. Cynically, one nurse manager noted that, al-though "nurses are very valuable, the sad thing is, we earn a huge amount of money, and why would you be impressed with a rep that brings you food from the local Chinese restaurant?" He suggested that nurses' experiences of being undervalued or having their work go unrecognized made them particularly susceptible to marketing initiatives that validated their work. "I think it's because outside the money," he surmised, nurses "don't get much, or they perceive they don't get much. So, anything like that is kind of like a bonus."

For nurses, it was rarely about the money or *personal* gain. Rather, industry has tapped into a more intangible form of appreciation that resonates deeply; taken a step further, industry also created work-arounds nurses could channel directly back into patient care, per-haps their greatest source of validation.

Addressing the Mismatch

When it came to interactions between nurses and industry, the effects of the "as-if" world of nursing played out in a range of ways. For some, marketing was benign and therefore devoid of risk, as the rejection of the identity of "decision maker" meant there was simply no possibility for undue influence, as in Lorraine's case. For others, marketing was particularly seductive, being one of the few places that nurses' expertise and authority were explicitly recognized. Others, however, actively challenged the "as-if" myth, asserting the power and influence of nurses and vigilantly monitoring interac-tions with industry in clinical spaces in order to protect patients.

Certainly sexism, the undervaluing of caring practices, and the historic, strategic subordination of the nursing profession by the medical profession and hospitals[7-9] all contribute to attitudes about the power nurses exercise. The as-if phenomenon is reminiscent of "medical etiquette" from the nursing profession's early history, when nurses' comportment and work routines were structured around physician dominance.[8] Yet nurses' accounts of decisions they made reveal that the physician "order" in many cases is more a product of *collective* decision making; for example, the nurses on Michelle's unit acquiring blanket orders on every patient, which they could execute at their discretion, or Vera's "remote" influence on the purchase of big-ticket items.

The nursing profession in the United States, through the recent revision of the Code of Ethics for Nurses,[10] acknowledges nurses as decision makers. The old Code of Ethics, published in 2001, stated that "the nurse is responsible and accountable for individual nursing practice and determines the appropriate delegation of tasks consistent with the nurse's obligation to provide optimum patient care," suggesting that a nurse's authority was relegated to the limits of nursing practice or to delegating to those with lesser power or authority.[11] The revised code, put out in 2015, now explicitly asserts a conception of nurses' power that includes autonomous decision making and characterizes nurses as leaders: "The nurse has authority, accountability, and responsibility for nursing practice; makes decisions; and takes action consistent with the obligation to promote health and provide optimal care."[10]

Nevertheless, the rhetoric contained in the newly revised Code of Ethics for Nurses, as well as discourses around multidisciplinary models of healthcare, remain mismatched with the as-if world many nurses still work in.[12] Rather than emulating physicians and striving for hierarchical and often oppressive "autonomy," nurses need to deconstruct the notion that prescribers are the only "decision makers" in clinical practice. The "prescription" and the "order" are collective, participatory processes, and the contributions of all participants need to be made visible and validated institutionally.

Many nurses in this study struggled with the mismatch between a complex and autonomous practice and a medicolegal culture that made their power and authority invisible. Industry understands this and is consequently inclusive with its marketing, making sure to touch upon anyone who might come into contact with its products down the pipeline. The tactic of exploiting hierarchies and validating those within its ranks is not new. Primary care providers, for example, are often flattered in ways that make them feel as valuable as specialists, who tend to make much more money and are often treated with greater respect.

Nurses and their labor continue to be perceived by healthcare institutions principally as a cost,[12] and some suggest that the invisibility of nursing work is a consequence of an economic model that has no way to quantify the "value" of nurses' work.[5] There is another fiction here: that the nurse's role and professional culture are truly valued. The reality is, professionals who are genuinely valued have control over the circumstances under which they practice. But hospitals provide recognition for nurses only—if at all—in the form of cheap trinkets on "Nurse Appreciation Day." These pale in comparison to what industry can provide; thus nurses are in a particularly susceptible position when it comes to interactions with reps or exposure to marketing. In a study of senior staff nurses in New Zealand, many reported receiving gifts and payments and justifying them in terms of perceived equity, explaining, "But doctors do it," as well as citing nurses' limited access to nonindustry educational resources or work tools.[13]

When it comes to industry, the as-if myth puts nurses at risk for conflicts of interest. In the as-if world, interacting with industry was a validating experience and was also perceived, often incorrectly, as ethically benign. As patient advocates, nurses need to both assert their leadership, yet be conscious of and vigilant about marketing in clinical spaces. With this in mind, in the next chapter I present profiles of nurses who navigated marketing interactions in their practice, and the ways they took a stand against commercial influence in clinical care.

chapter 5

"There Are Rules of Engagement"

Creating a Moral Space within Healthcare

Near the end of an interview with Maria, an infection control nurse at a public hospital, I asked what had motivated her to participate in the study. She explained that interacting with industry representatives had always been a part of the nursing role. However, she had never received any formal preparation for this part of her job.

"There are good and bad vendors, like everybody else," she reflected, recounting stories from her decades of practice, first in the operating room, then in infection control. "And there are rules of engagement, and there are some vendors that I am very PC with and there are others . . . where there's this trust factor."

Maria's rules of engagement were her own, developed through her experience and learning from the experiences of her mother, who had also been an operating room nurse; "listening to people who had been dealing with vendors for years; and then having a couple close calls myself."

Although Maria's hospital had a policy on interactions with sales representatives, it did not factor highly into the way that Maria navigated these relationships. She was not alone—many of the nurses I spoke with vaguely referred to the hospital's policy as the basis for how they approached interactions with industry, but most admitted they had not read the policy in detail or that they were unsure whether it applied to them as nurses. Clara, a pediatric staff nurse, summed it up: "I never really felt it affected me that much, that I had to necessarily read the fine print. I'm just vaguely kind of aware that I should not be taking quote-unquote bribes from companies. But because I'm not prescribing," she explained, "it never really seemed to affect me directly."

Part of having only a vague awareness of hospital policies on industry relations and conflicts of interest might stem from the work of the "as-if" myth—as Clara pointed out, since she was not prescribing, perhaps there was nothing at stake. Beyond this, however, and perhaps more importantly, it also stemmed from the fact that the policy did not reflect the realities of Clara's life as a staff nurse. Certainly, no company representative had ever offered her anything nice or expensive enough to count as a "bribe." At most, they had passed out some mini chocolate bars after the last in-service on a skin product for removing adhesive tape.

In fact, all of the hospitals I visited had a policy that prohibited staff from receiving gifts from industry, banned drop-in sales visits, and restricted the provision of free samples or product information. However, all of the policies also sanctioned the presence of sales reps with appointments for activities deemed to be in line with the hospital mission, including product in-services, product presentations to purchasing committees, and technical device support. The focus of the hospital policies was consequently largely risk management, stipulating that reps wear proper identification, observe patient confidentiality, and possess the necessary health and safety certifications. These policies failed to acknowledge the challenges associated with working with sales reps who, unsurprisingly, performed sales activities while present in the hospital in their sanctioned capacity. Because nurses were not directly addressed by hospital disclosure policies directed at clinical faculty or supply chain managers, their industry speaking engagements, drug dinner attendances, sponsored travel, and consulting arrangements were unknown to administrators. Nor did they receive any guidance for their day-to-day interactions with industry—interactions that administrators had approved.

For people like Maria, these policies did not address the kinds of situation she had identified as "close calls." Maria's rules of engagement instead were centered on a "trust factor": whether Maria could trust a company representative or whether she had to treat him or her with a heavy measure of distance depended on the person. "I started out trusting everybody, and then I realized, you can't do that. You've got to be suspicious. Because they're in it, it's their paycheck, and they get paid by commission." Maria had learned, sometimes the hard way, that sales reps' interests were not always aligned with what was best for patients or the hospital. These were the "close calls"—had things gone differently, a patient would have been in danger. In her field, this could be as serious as exposing a patient to an infection because of a faulty product or false promises.

The trust factor that Maria referenced was based not on principles, but on intuition and experience. It could not be summed up in a checklist or verified through documentation—vaccination certificates, criminal records checks—but grew out of Maria's relationships with reps. In contrast to a rational, explicit application of policy or ethical principles to daily practice, nurses instead described the often subtle feelings that arose in the course of their interactions with industry that suggested they had crossed into moral territory. Rather than a conscious realization, nurses described a gut reaction, such as "it just felt slimy to me," or "there's something not right."[1]

For some nurses, these relationships with industry provoked strong feelings, often ambivalence, which one nurse described as a "love-hate" relationship.[1] This ambivalence stemmed from the recognition that hospitals had initiated systemic cuts—particularly to continuing education, health promotion initiatives, and patient support—in an effort to increase the efficiency and decrease the costs associated with care delivery. Paradoxically, this has left nurses dependent on industry to deliver these services.[1]

The nurses who developed rules of engagement to guide their interactions with industry were responding to gut feelings. Not everyone had these feelings, and not everyone who did translated them into a set of practices. These gut feelings served as moral red flags that something important was at stake, be it the nurses' professional boundaries, the hospital budget, or the safety of a patient.[2] Nurses who reflected on these gut feelings sometimes translated them into a set of moral principles that guided their behavior when interacting with sales reps and how they managed the behavior of reps in clinical spaces.

In this chapter, I introduce a handful of nurses who developed their own rules of engagement, which were enacted on a personalized, ad hoc basis, often filling in the gaps left by formal policies and processes. These practices were grounded in each individual's practice and developed through their experiences, but they were wholly informal, differing among individuals and largely invisible at the level of the institution. Their experiences show that recognizing that interactions with industry are an ethical problem cannot be taken for granted.

For a minority of nurses I interviewed, their interactions with industry were morally significant in that they perceived these relationships to have implications for the well-being of patients, the hospital, or even the greater public, construed as taxpayers. For these nurses, the relationship was ethically problematic, and they sensed an inherent threat. This sense of threat, which enabled the identification of these interactions as morally significant, also prompted the development of rules of engagement, designed to manage these interactions in such a way as to mitigate the potential for ethical and sometimes physical or financial harm.

To illustrate how diverse these "rules" could be, I present a series of different practices that nurses used to manage their interactions with industry: policing, bargaining, skepticism, and vigilance. These are, of course, not the only ways that nurses navigated their interactions with industry, and they are not intended to judge these practices as right or wrong. Instead, I argue that our current policies for managing interactions with industry fall short of providing nurses with the language to articulate their ethical concerns, fail to validate nurses' ethical feelings, and do not make explicit what is at stake in the course of industry interactions. As it stands, it is left up to individual nurses to safeguard clinical spaces from marketing influence, which allows industry to divide and conquer, leaving patient care highly vulnerable.

Policing

"I'm kind of the 'compliance person guardian angel' related to vendors in the operating room," said Cassie, introducing herself. "And it's a pretty ugly job." She explained that the operating room probably saw more sales reps than anywhere else in the hospital—it wasn't unusual on any given day for five, six, seven reps to be in the operating rooms giving consultative information to physicians, as well as "god knows who trolling around trying to sell things."

"I can explain to you the vendor policy, and I can explain to you what the challenges are," she offered. Because of the particular vulnerability of patients in the operating room—to breaches of privacy and dignity, and to infection—many hospitals like Cassie's had, or were in the process of developing, more specific and restrictive rules to govern sales reps' access to and conduct within these restricted areas of the hospital. Cassie had made it her mission to enforce these department-specific rules in day-to-day practice through policing practices. While using institutional policy as a justification for enforcing particular comportment among clinical staff and sales reps, nurses like Cassie, however, had no real authority to levy consequences for a breach of the rules. Therefore, these nurses had to be highly vigilant in terms of enforcing the rules and protecting patients in case of a breach, always on alert and the defensive.

The job of policing vendors, Cassie explained, frequently felt "ugly" and was "annoying," both in that policing was required despite the apparent clarity and simplicity of the "rules" and in the unpleasant nature of the practice itself. In Cassie's eyes, sales reps, as technical experts, were meant to have a very specific and limited function. "They can sit in a corner and look cute. And when it's time, if they have a product they have to set up, they can set it up," she asserted. "But the moment the patient rolls in that door, they no longer can touch their piece of equipment. They can say to the nurse, 'Press that button,' . . . or 'Do this,' and that's what they're there for." According to Cassie, this hardline vis-à-vis sales reps came from her experience that they "constantly, constantly pushed the edge," acting outside of this scope, by answering the phone, using hospital computers, assisting nurses to open sterile packaging, or conducting sales speeches by the handwashing sinks. Some staff enabled and encouraged many of these behaviors.

Cassie expressed the "phenomenal pressure" she and staff nurses were under when policing vendor conduct. Often the vendor was present in the clinical area at the surgeon's behest and was thus allied with the most powerful individual in the operating room. Further, policing vendors often required violating social norms. The staff came to know sales reps over time; reps often joined staff functions or attended Christmas parties, so there was a social element in addition to the service relationship. Because sales reps in general were perceived to be friendly and helpful, confronting those who did not comply with the rules or who stepped outside the boundaries of their specific service role was construed as aggressive and rude by vendors and clinicians alike. Cassie characterized her attempts to confront vendors as "being the bitch," whether this was asking extra reps to leave the operating room to comply with the policy of one rep per room (to decrease infection risk), throwing out cups of coffee that reps brought into sterile operating rooms, or admonishing staff who relied on reps to tie their sterile gowns when colleagues were busy.

Cassie came down hard on reps and her colleagues, not because she had some inherent bias against the reps but because she, too, had had a number of close calls—as Maria did—that made it difficult for her to trust them to act appropriately. One Saturday morning, Cassie was at home unpacking groceries when she got a call from a staff nurse at the hospital. As the department's nurse educator, Cassie was on call for staff nurses if there was a situation they weren't sure how to manage. The nurse explained that she had been prepping for the morning case when a rep came into the operating room accompanied by "someone who looked rather young, with a vendor badge on." The staff nurse on duty noticed that the badge was flipped over, so she asked the vendor, "Oh, who's this?" The vendor told the nurse, "Oh, I'm training so-and-so." Cassie would have preferred that the nurse had drawn the line right there and asked the younger rep to leave because the hospital required that patients provide written consent for trainees to be present during their surgery.

The nurse on the phone explained that just a little while later she had been setting up the medical record for the procedure and needed to record the names of everyone who would be present during the case. She asked the young rep for his identification but halfway through entering the details, had stopped because she recognized the name she was typing, and the young rep in front of her wasn't that person. The staff nurse had cornered the older rep and, pointing to the younger one, demanded, "Who is he?" It turned out that the young "rep" was actually the sales rep's son, whom he had brought in on a quiet Saturday because the son wanted to see a surgery. The rep had borrowed a badge from one of his colleagues to get his son through the door. The staff nurse immediately had the child leave—the young rep turned out to be only about 17 years old—and called Cassie right away. Cassie was relieved that the nurse had been smart enough to figure out what was going on and to respond before the case began. Over the phone, she told the nurse to fill out an incident report, which she would handle on Monday.

Monday morning, Cassie contacted Materials Management and said, "I want to file a complaint. An incident report is going through. I've called Compliance already and Risk Management, but this rep needs to be suspended." Later that week, however, Cassie passed the same rep in the hallway. She was frustrated, explaining, "I don't know what they did. I have no clue, but I ratcheted it up to all the people, and if nothing else, I scared the hell out of the vendor."

Cassie applauded this nurse's detective skills and her assertiveness in dealing with a situation that had major safety and privacy implications. More commonly, however, nurses were reluctant to assert themselves, Cassie explained, knowing that "the doctor will get ticked because the rep is a friend of the doctor's." The staff nurses would either overlook the rep's behavior or call Cassie to address the situation on their behalf, again necessitating that she take on policing behaviors, challenging clinical hierarchies and violating social norms.

She lamented that the rep who had brought in his son had not been banned from accessing the operating room and that he was permitted to go about his business as usual, her satisfaction restricted to believing that he had been reprimanded through the incident-reporting process. Nurses who tried to police these interactions had no real authority to enforce institutional rules. They could file complaints or report reps to the supply chain department, but ultimately, it was not within their power to restrict a rep's access to the department or to have the rep banned from the institution. Nurses like Cassie could only revert to calling actual "police"—uniformed and armed institutional security—to have the rep temporarily escorted out of the clinical area. Cassie described the supply chain department at her hospital as a "weak link," and, as in the example above, she perceived that few consequences were ever levied when she made complaints about specific reps, even when patients were put at risk.

Nurses who took on policing practices became locked in a game of cops and robbers, understanding that reps "know what the rules are, so they work around the corner, and the staff either choose not to get it or don't get it because they haven't gotten punished yet." Unfortunately, the focus on enforcing rules created a sharp dichotomy, in which it sometimes seemed as though the robbers were Cassie's own colleagues.

One afternoon, a rep, on his way to a case, brought in a big plate of cookies for the staff and went to leave it in the break room. Knowing the hospital's policy that prohibited staff from receiving gifts from sales reps, Cassie intercepted the rep and told him, "We can't accept those. So you can take them, and give them to another hospital, or, if you hand them to me, I have to give them to Guest Relations, and they'll give them to patients." An hour later, she saw the same sales rep in the office of one of the nurse managers, and the same cookies being passed around to staff. Feeling undermined, Cassie confronted the manager, reasserting the hospital policy against gifts, but was made to feel unreasonable and overbearing.

For Cassie, the ugliness of the compliance piece of policing and the discomfort she experienced were overshadowed by the importance of her role as an advocate, which she believed was so integral to her nursing work that the pressures of violating social norms and power relations had to be weathered. As a nurse, Cassie was uniquely positioned to protect the interests of the patient, particularly in a space like the operating room, where patients' vulnerability was heightened, and typical advocates, like family members, were absent. However, Cassie invoked institutional policy as justification for her policing rather than the ethics of advocacy, because she was not institutionally empowered to truly advocate in the sense of levying consequences for behaviors that put a patient or the institution at risk. The whole purpose of the policy—ensuring safe clinical environments and patients' privacy—disappeared behind the rules, and no longer appeared relevant to many of Cassie's colleagues. Yet nurses like Cassie willingly carried the stigma of policing because they believed strongly that they were the patients' last line of defense.

Bargaining

Joel was the nurse manager of several intensive care units (ICUs) at a public academic medical center and was responsible for more than 300 employees. I met him in his office located on the unit, tucked just behind the nurses' station. As a nurse manager, Joel straddled the worlds of direct patient care and of management. He was responsible for the quality of care on the unit—interceding in emergencies, consulting on clinical situations—as well as the business of running a department—financial and personnel matters and the implementation of institutional policy.[3] Joel was responsible for his unit's budget, in the hundreds of thousands of dollars, and for keeping up with best practices in critical care, an area with rapid technological development. Interacting with sales representatives was thus a significant part of his job, though one that fluctuated in terms of time commitment, depending on the number of projects Joel had under way at a given time.

When I interviewed him, Joel was in the middle of negotiations to purchase a new bladder scanner for each of the ICUs he managed, at a cost of about $15,000 apiece. Having done this type of negotiation for a while, Joel had a few tactics up his sleeve. When they'd identified the need to upgrade their bladder scanners, he'd called the company rep, arranged a meeting, and asked the rep to get back to him with a quote. "What I do," Joel explained, "is get a quote for one machine and I never tell them that I'm going to buy more than one." Then, after sitting with the quote for a week or so, Joel called the rep again and said, "Well, I need a quote for three machines, and not at this price." Joel had learned that otherwise, the rep would give him the highest listed price. "So it's pretty interesting," he reflected, "because when you tell them that it's more than one machine, the price drops significantly."

At this stage, Joel had negotiated the price down to $12,000 per scanner. When I asked how he had learned to negotiate in this way, he talked about his time working as an accountant in the fast-food industry and all the lessons learned, which had transferred nicely into this aspect of his role as a nurse manager.

Joel, and others I interviewed, had acquired business savvy through past professional lives outside of nursing that translated to and were bolstered by experiences in nursing management. These nurses had invested a significant amount of time learning the language and practices of business and had adopted tactics from the business world, understanding that industry played by its own rules. They sought to level the playing field by engaging sales representatives on their own terms. Common among managers who must balance the administrative and clinical aspects of their role,[3] nurses like Joel experienced an ethical tension when bargaining with industry representatives that detracted from what they saw as their greater purpose—running a unit in the service of patient care.

"The first price that you'll always get from the rep is never the price. So it's kind of like buying a used car," Joel laughed, ironically. In making the analogy to used car sales, Joel juxtaposed nursing, the most trusted profession, with one of the least trusted occupations, car salespeople.[4] Underpinning Joel's bargaining tactics was the understanding that the information sales reps provided could not be taken at face value—this was just how the game was played. But for Joel, there was the threat of being taken advantage of in terms of price or quality, which impacted his budget and ultimately the quality of care his units could deliver.

In his references to the experience of buying a used car, Joel suggested that sales reps did not always play fairly, and he frequently spoke of sales reps "not meeting expectations" of directness or knowledgeability, or else "overpromising" the product's safety or efficacy, or more basically, of the company's ability to deliver the volume specified in the purchasing contract. Joel engaged in bargaining with a wry sense of humor, yet he also expressed, "It's very frustrating because nothing that you ever get is really, truly the price that you're talking about. It's pretty funny." This frustration stemmed from having to expend seemingly unnecessary time and energy in these negotiations before clinical and purchasing needs could actually be met. Thus, Joel had developed strategies around his industry interactions to best protect his time. "I am so busy that I hardly ever see someone who doesn't have an appointment with me," he explained. "My standard answer to them is, 'Leave me some information and if I'm interested, I'll call you and make an appointment.'"

In fact, Joel had a formula for playing hard to get that he used every time he was interested in buying a product. "My strategy for each rep is pretty similar—if I've made a contact for them . . . I will send them an email, then I will follow up with a phone call . . . I will ask for a sample." Once these three steps were in place, then, Joel explained "I won't communicate with them for two or three weeks, whether I'm highly interested or not because I don't want them to think that I'm eager." Joel did not want to invite the enthusiasm that often accompanied the promise of a sale, which included a barrage of follow-up emails, calls, visits, samples, and offers of education, support—extras meant to entice. Rather, "when you're bringing in a product," Joel urged, "people need to realize that it should never be an emergency, unless it's truly something life-threatening—which it shouldn't be."

This formula, like a complex game of dating, allowed Joel to regulate the progression, and extent of the relationship with the sales rep, and to adequately vet a product. "Everything needs to be thought out really slowly," he reflected. "Take your time, and then make contacts with other people who are using the products to see what are the pros and what are the cons." Joel attempted to strike a balance between beating industry reps at their own game and not diverting too much time and attention away from his clinical work and other management roles. Although effective for Joel in terms of negotiating what he deemed to be a fair price for a high-quality piece of equipment, this process took concentration, deliberateness, and significant time and effort—and this was just one little project that Joel had on his plate.

Behind these tactics and strategies was an attempt by Joel and others to hold companies and their sales reps accountable for the cost, and quality of their products and services. The only way these nurses thought they could leverage enough power to do so was to adopt bargaining tactics such as competition and boycotts. John, formerly a nurse manager, was now directing a major hospital renovation. He took a hard line on any interaction he had with industry, and over the years he had adopted aggressive tactics in his work to hold companies accountable. For John, one particular incident had crystallized for him the stakes of these interactions. In the mid-2000s, John was involved in purchasing an X-ray machine from a US-based multinational conglomerate that captured images in real-time. The X-ray was used during surgeries, such as a metal rod insertion for a bone fracture, in which it provided a dynamic image of the actual insertion. The machine began causing problems when clinicians noticed that when they "put the image in one patient's name, it would end up with another patient's name on it," or that the image was no longer "live," which, John explained, "is a huge issue." "Because if you think it's live and you're pushing in the rod, you've pushed it in too far, causing more damage to the patient."

When John reported these malfunctions to the company, the company denied any product failure. "So we complained to the company, and they said, No, no, no. There's nothing wrong with our machines: it's your electricity that's fluctuating.'" In response, the hospital ordered a battery of electricity tests and purchased a generator that would regulate any irregular electricity flows. After this major expense, the Food and Drug Administration recalled all of these X-ray machines and halted their manufacture; it turned out that these problems were popping up worldwide. John and his team arranged a meeting with the company directors to request that they shoulder the cost of renting machines for the hospital from another company, believing that it should take responsibility not only for the product failure but also for the cover-up. The company directors, however, refused. John was disgusted by the response, believing that a healthcare company ought to have some concern for their ultimate consumers, patients. "The sad thing is—I don't think they care anything about patients. It's all about money."

About a decade later, John was in charge of a multibillion-dollar hospital renovation. He decided to take a page from industry's play-book: he would enact a hospital-wide boycott on all that company's products, having lost all trust both in their products and their accountability. "Nothing in the whole building," he promised, "I don't care if it's a sink. Take out everything. We've got the backing of the doctors too. The company has lost millions and millions and millions and millions of dollars for it. And it's not to be spiteful. It's about patient safety. It's about us surviving as a hospital. And it's the right thing to do for the taxpayers." John felt sick about the company's conduct, an experience that stayed with him through his career and sensitized him to what was at stake when interacting with company representatives, who were pursuing goals that were potentially in conflict with his own.

Nurses who adopted bargaining tactics were frequently in a position like John's and Joel's—they recognized that, not only was the well-being of an individual patient perhaps at stake when a product failed, but the financial health of the hospital and, in the case of a public institution, the wider community, as taxpayers, could also be threatened in the course of these dealings. Although the shady feeling of buying a used car or the sense of disgust emanated directly from their practice, the nurses struggled to find the authority to address these moral dilemmas. Instead, they borrowed strategies from the business world in an attempt to negotiate fairly, though frequently at the expense of their limited time and energy.

Skepticism

Mark approached his interactions with industry with what he called a "real paranoia." The gut feeling that industry interactions contained an element of threat was elevated to the level of deep distrust. Mark had a heightened sense of ambivalence toward industry interactions because, like other participants, he was highly reliant on industry resources, yet questioned their bias and integrity. Mark was a clinical nurse specialist, based in the Medical-Surgical Department at a public hospital. His focus was on sepsis, the body's inflammatory response to an infection, which is the leading cause of death and the most expensive illness to treat among hospitalized patients.[5] Like Rachel in Chapter 3, Mark also had something of an impossible job: he was responsible for consulting on all patients at risk for or diagnosed with sepsis in the entire hospital, providing sepsis-related education to staff nurses, selecting and implementing products to assist in the prevention and treatment of sepsis, and performing surveillance and tracking on sepsis cases. He often had to turn to industry representatives for assistance in providing training to nursing staff or researching new products, but unlike Rachel, he was deeply skeptical of this help.

Before becoming a nurse, Mark had worked in advertising, representing companies who wished to purchase advertising space, a job in which he interacted with sales reps selling ad space on a daily basis. He possessed a keen understanding of the intent and mechanisms of marketing and its powerful, often subconscious effects. "Because I controlled these budgets, I was also advertised very heavily to, and so that whole industry was all about the fancy nights out," he recalled. "They'll take you to a club or whatever. I saw a Madonna concert for free." But in healthcare, Mark believed, the stakes were higher. Advertising is "an industry where no one's life is at stake. I thought it was kind of sleazy then," he reflected, "but it was very overt, so it was very interesting to come to the medical world and see that the same stuff happens." His past life in advertising had primed Mark's awareness of the potential for the introduction of bias into clinical decision making. But his awareness stemming from his insider experiences selling and buying ad space was escalated to a level of paranoia within the context of healthcare, where people's lives and safety were at stake.

The paranoia stemmed partially from Mark's reliance on sales representatives to help him train the staff on new products, and he did not see a way around his dependence on their resources. On the one hand, Mark explained, having sales representatives deliver this education "made sense," partly due to the rep's expertise in the particular product, but also because Mark's team did not "have the man power to do it." For Mark, however, relying on industry reps was a precarious trade-off, and he needed to be ever wary that the cost of using industry resources was not too high.

In Mark's experience, sales reps used these training opportunities to subtly introduce related, branded products, which made him uncomfortable and provoked his sense of distrust. "There's this real obligation on our part to make sure that we know what the reps are saying, and that we have some influence on that," referring to his colleagues in nursing education and the unit managers. "And it can be difficult to do. It can be difficult to say, 'When I'm not here, don't you tell anyone that the Hospira tube-feeding or whatever is better than the other, because there's actually no evidence to say that.' It's very hard to—you can't actually control that." The dilemma for Mark was that what the sales rep presented carried the institution's endorsement, and staff nurses assumed that Mark had vetted the content of the in-service. He recognized that whatever the sales rep presented would become practice within the institution once nurses began to integrate the education with their practice. But as he pointed out, unless he was physically present—and the whole point of engaging industry was because Mark *could not* always be physically present—there was no way he could be sure the reps stayed on message and true to the evidence.

Mark's "on-guardness," as he put it, came from knowing that reps were "not going to give you all the information. They're going to give you information that proves their point." Mark recalled an industry presentation that "on the face of it," he remembered, appeared "very, very sophisticated and very educational about, for example, wound care products, trying to encourage us to use more silver-impregnated methyl cellulose foam for wound packing instead of other competing products." The presentation, he recalled, seemed so impressive because it was "full of references and full of scientific evidence." But as he and his colleagues sat through the talk, questions arose. Someone raised a hand and asked, "Well, okay, you have this reference. Let's talk about that reference. Like, what were they actually looking at?" Mark realized that the reps often were not able to answer these more pointed questions, and they frequently left out key details. One of his colleagues in the room happened to have read the study in question and brought it into the staff room the next day. As they read through the research study, they realized that the rep had omitted the fact that there was little to no evidence to support the product choice. Having the skills to critically appraise scientific evidence and to have a critical, questioning mindset seemed vital to Mark: "There are people who are very well-prepared to make those determinations, and there are people who are still developing those skills. And I think that it's an urgent need, given the onslaught of advertising that we've already described."

While nurses like Joel, who engaged in bargaining, were unwilling to take sales reps at their word in the course of negotiations, instead employing tactics in an attempt to achieve fairness, Mark questioned all of the information provided by industry, as well as the influence industry might have over seemingly independent sources. His skepticism was grounded in the belief that the foundation of practice—the evidence underpinning the techniques, products and equipment used in the course of nursing care—was threatened by industry's involvement. While Mark's skepticism was intended to detect bias and influence within his practice, the paranoia stemmed from understanding that, while deeply appreciating what was possibly at stake, he could perhaps never find a truly objective source of information.

Mark remarked upon the "lack of skepticism" that he observed in the nursing profession and among his colleagues, giving as an example the "*real* enthusiasm" he observed when people talked about pharmaceutical-sponsored dinners they had attended. He was troubled that these colleagues did not even have a hint of wondering, "Should I have any questions about this? I'm sort of being advertised to. I'm kind of renting my brain and giving myself the opportunity to be *unduly* influenced." Mark noted that everybody believes himself or herself to be immune to advertising, "I mean, I probably do it my-self," he acknowledged. "'Other people are susceptible but I'm not,' is how everyone thinks about advertising, right? *'I'm* smart enough to know the difference, and I won't be influenced, but other people will.' But of course, we all are." Mark stressed the subtlety of mar-keting interactions and how insidious marketing activities could be, underscoring the need to "pay attention" to the possibility that bias might enter one's practice.

For nurses like Mark, questioning was at the heart of their inter-actions with industry. Feeling like a form of resistance, question-ing was a way to continue interacting with industry without feeling compromised by the interaction. At other times, being physically present was the only way to monitor sales reps' interactions with staff nurses. Being present, however, was very challenging for peo-ple like Mark, who could not perform the staff education with the hospital resources available; industry representatives were vital to these activities.

Instead, Mark attempted to "do his own homework," which in-volved reading the full studies rather than just the abstracts or bul-let points circulated by sales reps, performing his own literature review, and validating presentation content in advance. "People in positions like mine," Mark explained,

> are tasked, oftentimes, with trying to make these complicated eval-uations of equipment or products and things like that, whether it's a wound care product—I mean, it could be a million different things, and it's a really challenging job to sift through practical experiences that other hospitals have had and the needs of our particular patients and our particular hospital, the research that's out there about how effective something is or isn't—it's a big job.

Mark might also be evaluating multiple products at a given time, and he found that these processes could easily overwhelm his other responsibilities. But just like a "perfect friend," Mark found that "vendors are frequently *very* available to help with that process and provide all kinds of information . . . It feels in the moment like it's making the job a lot easier." However, as Mark pointed out, the generosity of sales reps often doubled his workload, as he was responsible not only for doing his own homework but also for vetting the information the rep provided. For Mark, his "paranoia" stemmed from believing that the marketing occurred covertly: the unfavorable studies of the product omitted from presentations, the subtle sales pitch tucked into an educational offering, the sales speech delivered when he was not in attendance.

Mark felt the need to be so cautious because he often found he was addressing these issues alone. The nursing profession rarely had conversations about interacting with industry. He also noted that there had been nothing about interacting with industry in his master's program. At his institution, he perceived that nurses "don't really know about the policies a lot of times." He had witnessed "people in this hospital who have lunch brought in by vendors—sit and have lunch and get a presentation, and it's actually against policy, and no one really talks about it. Or I don't think they know. I really don't think that they know. I don't think anyone's trying to break any rule."

He had been involved several years earlier with planning a local conference. At the last minute, the organizers were scrambling after a couple of speakers had dropped out. In their place, someone invited people to speak about specific products—one was a sales rep, another worked on industry-sponsored research. Mark was the only person to note that the organization, or at least its local chapter, had no history of requiring that speakers disclose their relationships with industry. When he urged the organizers to look into it, they found nothing in the bylaws or other professional standards related to disclosing conflicts of interest. "But it was a really awkward thing," Mark remembered, because the suggestion was not welcomed.

This surprised Mark, especially because of the recent attention to physicians' relationships with industry and public disclosure, leaving him to feel that nursing was "still kind of behind." Mark suggested that his colleagues were not acting unethically, but rather that they did not perceive that attending a sponsored lunch was an ethical situation. In pointing to the silence around industry interactions in terms of educational preparation, policy implementation, and professional discourse, Mark described a particular moral space,[2] or sociopolitical climate, that fostered silence rather than the kind of attunement Mark embodied. Thus, the import and the ethical aspects of industry interactions, which were so apparent to Mark, receded for those working in this kind of moral space.

Vigilance

For Maria, the patient's safety was at the heart of everything she did. "As far as my role as infection control," said Maria, "we think of this as the original patient safety organization. We've always done the same thing, which is, basically, keep the patient safe, make sure that everything we use on them is safe to use." Her job involved not only clinical issues, such as isolating patients with infectious diseases, immunizing, and preventing the spread of germs, but also ensuring the cleanliness of the facility, including sterilizing instruments and cleaning equipment. She was a key voice on the hospital's purchasing committee, which needed to factor in how new products would be cleaned and disposed of before signing a contract. This position, and the follow-up that needed to occur for many products, brought her into frequent contact with sales representatives.

Maria used the phrase "rules of engagement" to describe how she approached these interactions. She stood out in that she named her interactions with industry as explicitly ethical in nature, describing them in terms of boundaries, trust, and conflict of interest. Maria embodied a state of vigilance because she set careful and deliberate boundaries in her relationships with reps in order to build and preserve trust, but always with the ultimate goal of keeping staff and patients safe. She positioned herself as a gatekeeper, to the facility in some ways, and particularly to her colleagues, monitoring reps' access to clinicians and vigilantly upholding the boundaries.

Maria began her career in the operating room, where she also interacted heavily with sales reps. "When I was in the OR, all those OR suppliers were young and attractive," she recalled. "And they had accounts, you know; the rules have changed over the past ten years, but they used to have spending accounts that were exorbitant." She remembered frequent offers, "Come, let's take you to lunch, let's take you to dinner." But Maria would always respond, "I don't think so, I just don't feel comfortable with that—thanks, but no thanks," attributing her discomfort to her "Catholic guilt factor." There was always a part of her that believed, "This can't be right. I should never be this friendly with somebody that's trying to have me buy a product." She set boundaries, not because it was in an official policy or because she had been taught to do so, but because her gut feeling told her to do so.

When Maria first started working in the operating room, she worked with two young male neurosurgeons. Part of her responsibilities dictated that she purchase supplies and equipment on their behalf. The sales reps, on the other hand, were "all these attractive women who would come in in short skirts and high heels, perfectly groomed, made up, everything gorgeous, and they would be selling all this stuff." One day she found that her purchasing budget had been depleted, so she confronted the surgeons.

"Guys, you've spent all of our money. You can no longer meet with vendors alone. You have to come through me, we'll meet with them as a team. You tell me why you want to meet with them, then we'll set it up and we'll have a whole thing." Maria, as guardian of the department's purchasing budget, decided she needed to be a gatekeeper for the sales reps' access to the surgeons, monitoring checks and balances along the way. The surgeons agreed: "Ok, well that makes sense."

Their first team meeting with the sales reps really put Maria off. The reps were talking comfortably and familiarly, exclusively to the surgeons. "I'm sorry, as a female it would bother me," referencing the flirtatious banter that went on throughout. "You could *see*," she remembered, "they were ignoring me and focusing the conversation on the surgeons, and you could tell that they had established a relationship and a rapport."

Midway through the sales pitch, one surgeon turned to Maria and asked, "Ok, how does this go? What do you think?"

Maria replied matter-of-factly, "It's too expensive. We've got the same device, you've not complained about it, so why are we looking at a new product for more cost when we're happy with what we've got?"

"Oh, you're right, you're right. We don't need to do that," the surgeon acknowledged.

After a few such meetings, Maria noted that the tide had turned. After about three months of these kinds of interaction, some new faces, which were decidedly more male, appeared to represent the products. The attention began to shift: Maria, whom the sales reps realized held the purse strings, was now the recipient of invitations to lunch and attempts to establish a relationship.

Maria held firm, "Noooo, you don't need to take me to lunch," she'd say. "I'm busy, what have you got? Show me your information, tell me why you're here, and I've got to move on." It was obvious to her, she said, that "they were trying to curry favor."

Maria found the need to act as a guardian not only of budgets, but of her colleagues and their time, as well. Sales reps in the hospital, often on other business, took every opportunity to bend an ear, hoping to spark some interest in a product and find a clinician interested enough to formally request a product or try out a free sample.

When Maria first took the job as an infection control nurse, she made a pact with the operating room staff. Sales reps routinely peppered the department with offers of new products to prevent infections at the surgical site, such as skin preparations. Maria offered, "I'm going to make you a deal. I will be the gatekeeper for these products. If at the end of a year I come back to you and say, I think we need to address these product needs, then we'll do it." The staff agreed not to talk to any sales reps, in an effort to keep the sales pitches and the free samples out of the department.

Right off the bat, Maria had four or five different companies calling her. "I just started working here," she explained to each rep. "I don't even know what's going on in the hospital, I don't know our rates of infection yet, I don't even know our OR manager. So, just don't call me. Let me get my feet in the water here." She set a boundary: "You can call me back in six months to a year. Because by *that* time, I will have established myself and I'll know what's going on." She reasoned that if there was a real problem with the infection rates or defective products, the OR staff would be knocking down her door, so she was confident that the products they had in place were doing the job.

All of the reps respected her request, except for one. He kept calling and calling and calling, leaving voicemails, sending emails. Finally, Maria called him back: "*I told* you, I don't know enough at this time to make a change. If you call me again you're going to make me mad. Don't do that. You have nothing new, I know your product. I'm familiar with it, I know how it works. We are okay."

Rather than respecting the limits Maria set, the rep decided to see if another clinician might be more receptive and began contacting and dropping in on staff in the operating room. This riled the staff, particularly the OR manager, who called Maria, exasperated, "I thought you were going to keep this guy away from us!"

Maria, feeling undermined, called the rep. "You're now going to have to prove *a lot* before I'm even going to want to talk to you again because what I asked for was not unreasonable, and you continued to go around and bother people." This sales rep had willfully circumvented Maria's role as gatekeeper and had compromised her ability to guard the staff and the facility from marketing influence. This behavior violated her trust in the rep, and consequently, in the rep's product, as Maria was skeptical that it would live up to this rep's promises regarding quality and safety. Because this vendor refused to acknowledge or respect the boundaries she had created, and then undermined her even further by circumventing her gatekeeping function, Maria was no longer willing to work with him in any capacity.

"So, there has to be a trust," she reflected. "And when reps violate that trust, it's like, we're all here to keep our patients safe, nobody's looking to favor one company over another. Whoever has the best product is who we're going to go with."

Even the perception of favoritism could call a product's value and efficacy into question. During one purchasing committee meeting, an operating room nurse presented a big-ticket surgical item they wanted to bring in. It was an orthopedic system, including a scope camera and shaver, used for arthroscopies, a type of minimally invasive joint surgery. The nurse presenting the product request was really excited about bringing it in and seemed to know a great deal about the product, urging the committee members, "This could be great."

"How do you know so much about this?" Maria asked out of curiosity.

"Well, they flew me out to their corporate headquarters in Colorado. They showed me around their company, showed me the factory, took me to dinner, we went on a skiing trip!"

"You did *what?*" exclaimed a number of the committee members. "What made you think that was okay?! There are rules against that." Accepting the paid travel and gifts of a ski trip and dinners was in direct contravention of the hospital's policy on conflicts of interest. In this case, the nurse nearly lost his job.

"You cannot have ANY question of partiality," Maria explained, particularly in the context of recommending and making decisions about purchasing. "Definitely there was now a question of favoritism because of what the nurse had done. He'd established this friendship and rapport with the company's reps and knew them all and called them all by first names." The committee members no longer had any faith in the product or its merits, believing the presentation—and even the need for the product—to have been exaggerated in favor of the company.

"I'm not the friend of a vendor. I may get to know some of them because of how they are at work, but we're not your friend. You're nice and we like you, but we're not your friends." This boundary remained at the forefront of Maria's interactions with reps. It's "a fine line to walk," she explained, because over time, she'd get to know reps that came to the hospital regularly, sometimes over the course of years.

Maria's rules of engagement sharply contrasted with the accounts of the sales reps as the "perfect friends" and with the assumption that these relationships could be win-win. Maria realized that even the perception of friendship between sales reps and clinicians could undermine trust in the products used in patient care and in the expertise of the clinician. Rather than succumbing to the collegial and even validating feelings that arise through friendships, Maria rejected these overtures because they triggered a sense that she had crossed into ethically problematic territory.

Building a Moral Space

For a handful of nurses in this study, interacting with industry carried an underlying sense of threat, which manifested as a gut feeling that something was not quite right. For those who engaged in policing, this threat was constant and overt, as they chased down reps violating hospital policy. For those who opted to bargain, the sense of threat was part of the game of doing business, and though less perplexing, required savvy to guard against being ripped off. For others, the threat was much more covert and subtle, requiring detective-like questioning and constant skepticism. Maria, in her vigilant campaign against infection, interpreted everything in terms of patient safety, and false promises or faulty products could put people at risk. The sense of threat popped up in a number of corners: whether a product was safe to use on a given patient, whether staff and their precious time were protected from needless sales pitches, and ultimately, whether the hospital or even the tax-paying public had to foot the bill for wasted time or products no one really needed.

Nurses took their gut feelings, however, and translated them into a highly diverse set of practices designed to mitigate the perceived threat. This diversity was largely the result of these practices being developed individually and on an ad hoc, experiential basis. Without judging any of these practices to be good or bad, diversity itself, however, could become a problem. Because nurses each approached their interactions with industry in different ways, sales reps could exploit the fragmentation, working through the cracks.

Sales representatives tailor their marketing strategies to individuals through systematically assessing and documenting clinicians' personalities, practice styles, and preferences.[6] When asked about the sales reps they liked to work with, these nurses responded consistently with the practices that they themselves had taken on:

those who policed appreciated reps who respected and abided by "the rules"; those who bargained liked "getting it straight," as John put it; Maria appreciated reps who respected her boundaries, who "make an appointment, call in advance, tell you what they've got, are already prepared to answer all your questions." However, with the growing size of sales territories and a tendency for reps to jump from company to company, creating a revolving door of sales reps, these nurses were often dealing with the exact same reps despite working in different hospitals.

Only a handful of nurses, however, perceived any sort of threat, and most approached their interactions with industry as routine, unproblematic, and even validating. The normalization of relationships with industry occurs in part because effective marketing generates a whole host of other, highly positive feelings. Surveys of doctors, nurses, and pharmacists describe the overwhelmingly positive feelings clinicians have toward industry representatives who are regarded as friendly, sociable, helpful, and knowledgeable about their products and marketing.[7-10] Sales reps are selected for their personable, outgoing natures and are trained to influence health professionals through "finely titrated doses of friendship,"[6] as was explored in Chapter 3. In Chapter 4, I showed that nurses experienced marketing as inclusive and validating. The provision of gifts, in particular, is a highly effective inducement to recommending, prescribing, or purchasing a product; receiving samples, pens, a coffee, dinner invitations, and speaking engagements induces powerful feelings of reciprocity and builds allegiance between health professionals and sales reps.[11,12]

Strategies to manage industry interactions that are targeted at individuals perpetuate the sense that clinicians can inoculate themselves against industry influence. As professionals trained in the sciences and committed to evidence-based practice, many commonly believe that they are capable of detecting bias by taking industry information with a "grain of salt," doing their own research, or even achieving a balanced perspective by meeting with sales representatives from multiple companies.[13] While educating clinicians is vitally important to create awareness about industry influence in clinical practice, the most effective solutions have been structural: bans on gifts, food, and visits from sales representatives.[14]

What is perhaps most concerning, however, is that nurses are working in contradictory environments. While hospital policies seek to control the flow of samples and cold calls, they also create officially sanctioned roles for sales representatives; interacting with marketers has become part of the job for many nurses. Physician researchers share this conundrum, reporting that their institutions strongly encourage industry collaboration, while administrating conflict of interest policies that result in blame to individuals caught up in compromising situations.[15] In both cases, the conditions under which these conflicts of interest or commercial influences arise are left unquestioned.[15]

It is thus not surprising that most health professionals fail to recognize the potential for conflicts of interest or the ethically problematic nature of relationships with industry. Nurses work within institutional climates that create and maintain invisibility around their interactions with industry, while simultaneously seeking to foster industry interactions in the interest of the hospital. This impossible work situation creates the conditions in which conflicts of interest are increasingly normalized and built into the very functioning of the hospital.

The Code of Ethics for registered nurses explicitly calls on nurses to "establish, maintain, and improve the ethical environment of the work setting and conditions of employment."[16] This mandate could be interpreted as a moral space, or a social and political climate that fosters moral awareness and perception,[2] such as attunement to the negative gut feelings that marketing provoked among some nurses in this study. To effectively address marketing influence within hospitals, nurses require a moral space that acknowledges that interactions with industry do occur, validates their feelings of unease as they arise, and empowers them to subsequently take moral action. This means formally preparing nurses for interacting with industry, officially recognizing the work that nurses do in managing these interactions, collectively enacting policies that ensure ethical boundaries are maintained, and banning gifts, food, and sales visits in professional practice. In the concluding chapter, I propose how we might begin creating a moral space in healthcare institutions that checks this pervasive commercial influence and safeguards the integrity of health professionals and the quality of patient care.

chapter 6

Marketing to Nurses Matters

How to Address Commercial Influence in Healthcare

Interactions between nurses and industry are commonplace in day-to-day clinical practice. Nurses encounter sales representatives, their marketing messages, samples, and gifts in the context of relationships that are deemed to be in the service of education or patient care. Understanding that nurses wield tremendous influence within hospitals and healthcare systems, pharmaceutical and medical device companies exhibit at nursing conferences, extend invitations to drug company-sponsored dinners, and enroll nurses as consultants and speakers.

Yet, paradoxically, these interactions remain invisible, particularly to healthcare leaders and certainly to the public. In this book I report on these interactions, attempting to understand the conditions under which these interactions are made and remain invisible and the implications they hold for the public interest.

Hospitals have created a strategic invisibility around nurse-industry interactions. This allows institutions to benefit from industry resources while externalizing the costs of industry interactions to the public and outsourcing their practical and ethical management to individual clinicians. Chapter 2 examines how hospitals have formalized many nurse-industry interactions through policy and procedures. While these policies purportedly curtail marketing in clinical spaces, they also create legitimate roles for sales representatives within day-to-day hospital care. These policies frequently displace marketing, so that it happens beyond the purview of the formal process, leaving individual clinicians vulnerable to influence. Thus, while hospital administrators generally denied that nurses interact with industry at all, nurses described multiple and diverse relationships with industry representatives, and marketers detailed their particular interest in forming such relationships.

Certainly, the power relations among nurses, physicians, and hospitals contribute to creating the conditions wherein nurses' frequent and varied interactions with industry can be made invisible and treated as benign. Nurses often felt validated when their expertise was recognized and valued by industry representatives and, at times, agreed to further industry's interests as the "inside man" (Chapter 3). Chapter 4 explores the as-if myth that permeates nursing practice and bolsters the widely held belief that marketing to nurses is harmless, given that clinicians who are "just" nurses do not make decisions in the absence of a doctor's order.

Nurses, however, also benefitted from the invisibility surrounding their interactions with industry, which allowed them to use industry resources as work-arounds to gaps in the system and to participate in marketing relationships, while feeling self-assured that these relationships were ethically benign. In fact, few nurses acknowledged interactions with industry to be an ethical problem; at most, these interactions constituted a relatively minor problem in comparison with the many ethical challenges of clinical practice. In these circumstances, industry resources seemed helpful and sometimes seemed to be the only way to address resource shortages and institutional constraints.

The invisibility cloaking nurse-industry interactions extended to the policy level both in hospitals and in state and federal sunshine laws. Either nurses were omitted from these mandates, or policies failed to directly address the issue of industry interactions within the context of nursing practice. Instead, in the course of practice, some nurses had developed personalized, ad-hoc "rules of engagement" to deal with industry representatives on their own, which left the system fragmented and open to exploitation (Chapter 5).

If policies continue to focus only on physicians or even prescribers and place the onus for managing interactions with industry on individuals, the entire system will remain vulnerable to commercial influence. Instead, addressing the effects of the commercialization of healthcare needs to be a collective endeavor.

Marketing is highly inclusive because industry cannot risk alienating anyone who might facilitate consumption of their product. Patients rely on prescribers to make a brand choice—not true for other consumer products—which is influenced by healthcare guidelines or constrained by insurers or hospital formularies.[1] A medication, for example, is prepared by a pharmacist and then administered by a nurse, both of whom might provide feedback to prescribers and monitor the patient's experience. The patient's experience in turn might be influenced by family members, friends, or the media. Industry must market to all of these groups as if they were consumers, given these multiple pathways of influence over the choice of product.[1] Whether it is an industry-sponsored event that includes health professionals from multiple disciplines,[2] treating the medical assistant in an orthopedic surgeon's office to an after-work happy hour,[3] or a strategic marketing plan that addresses every aspect of the product's distribution, from policy maker to insurer to clinician to patient,[1] industry does not discriminate in its attempts to influence.

An obvious and straightforward solution would be to include nurses in policies like the Sunshine Act. France and Australia, for example, require that companies disclose payments to all licensed health professionals.[4,5] Nurses, like their physician colleagues, serve as paid speakers and consultants and accept gifts. These relationships, too, need to be transparent so that their impact on healthcare and professional education can be evaluated.

However, determining how to address commercial influence within healthcare means we need to scrutinize the conditions that foster and normalize relationships between health professionals and the for-profit medical industry. Thinking about the interface between nurses and industry as a relationship between a company and an individual nurse ignores the reality that for many nurses, interacting with industry is part of their working life, sometimes by choice and sometimes by circumstance. The boundary between healthcare and industry is often blurry, given that healthcare has become big business.[6] Nurses work in hospitals that are either owned by corporations or that emulate the corporate business model, which makes it difficult to identify the line between healthcare and industry.[6]

I argue that we need to move beyond disclosure in changing the conditions under which health professionals interact with industry. This means addressing the corporatization of healthcare and thinking about conflicts of interest as a systemic issue. We need to debunk the myth that manufacturers of drugs and devices are an appropriate source of education about these products; we must call for the provision of product support that is independent of sales. Nurses are uniquely positioned to lead this challenge as members of the most trusted profession and of an independent, collective professional body. I propose a series of policy proposals to begin confronting the pervasive presence of commercial interests in clinical practice, while ensuring that nurses, as expert end users, contribute to the development of innovative healthcare products.

Beyond Disclosure

Disclosure is the most commonly proposed and implemented solution for dealing with the effects of conflicts of interest that can arise from relationships between health professionals and industry.[7] The Physician Payments Sunshine Act has now been in effect for several years, establishing a new era of transparency within medicine and healthcare in the United States with the creation of the Open Payments public database. Similar policies have been enacted in a number of other countries globally.[4,5] Although these disclosures paint a picture of the abundant financial relationships between physicians and industry, they fail to capture the extent to which sales representatives have become integrated into the day-to-day functioning of hospitals.

Without knowing about the kinds of interaction health professionals have with industry, it is impossible to know how to manage them.[8] Yet, disclosure itself doesn't address the real or perceived influence at work, nor does it protect decision making from bias.[8] Instead, disclosure of health professionals' ties to medically related industry allows us to understand the scope of industry's promotional activities. The Open Payments data will provide policy makers, journalists, and researchers with a clearer picture of the prevalence and nature of the financial relationships between physicians and the pharmaceutical and medical device industries. In this sense, the Sunshine Act is a notable advance toward greater transparency in healthcare.

Part of the impetus behind the sunshine legislation was the public's right to know, underpinned by the assumption that this knowledge would empower patients who might be affected by biased decision making.[9] Without judging any of these interactions as good or bad, the Centers for Medicare and Medicaid Services hoped that public reporting in itself would serve as a deterrent to relationships that are inappropriate, while allowing beneficial relationships to continue, with the public's knowledge and trust.[10]

The jury is still out, however, as to whether public disclosure of financial relationships between health professionals and industry is a deterrent or is empowering. A recent experiment found that patients rated physicians who received high value payments from industry as less honest and less committed to patients' best interests than those who did not accept any money.[11] Other experiments, however, have shown that disclosure can sometimes backfire, causing an advisor to increase the bias in their advice because they feel less guilty after disclosing their conflict.[12] In other cases, those receiving advice are sometimes more uncomfortable rejecting it when it is accompanied by a disclosure because it might signal that they do not trust the physician.[13] This means that disclosure might actually create a burden on those whom it was designed to empower.[7]

In those cases in which these relationships are more complex than an individual clinician receiving a payment or gift from a company, disclosure may be even more limited. Few members of the public realize the extent to which sales representatives are embedded—in operating rooms, cardiac catheterization labs, in-service education, and purchasing decisions—and what this might mean for their care. Simply disclosing the fact that sales representatives are present in clinical spaces, however, leaves patients and their families in a difficult position.

My 60-year-old Canadian father took the summer off to have a hip replacement. This being his second new hip, we were more confident, relieved that his burning joint pain was soon to end, and familiar with the surgeon who had replaced the other hip. Having been through this before, my parents had a shorter list of questions for his preoperation appointment with the surgeon, but I called my dad the night before the appointment to throw in my two cents. I urged my parents to ask the surgeon: "Is the sales representative for the hip implant company going to be in the operating room?"

When my parents sat down in the surgeon's office with a surgical resident observing in the corner, they posed my question. The surgeon responded affirmatively, that the sales representative for the hip implant would be present throughout the surgery, and he then launched into a firm explanation.

"No one knows the equipment like these guys," he told my parents, meaning the device representatives. "Sometimes the nurses are not familiar with everything that should be on the table," he explained. "These guys know their stuff and make sure everything is there. I used to come in on a Sunday night to set up the operating room and to make sure everything was accounted for. Now the rep does that for me," he recounted with some relief.

The surgeon told of a new era of accountability wherein the orthopedic surgeons monitored one another's expenditures, keeping costs down through this form of peer pressure, as if to allay fears that the presence of a sales representative in the operating room would lead to the promotion of increased use or use of more expensive implants. He explained that having sales reps in the operating room was a typical practice—all the orthopedic surgeons "had" a rep.

"We didn't want to push the issue, because what would we do? We wouldn't want to antagonize him before the surgery!" my mother sighed at the end of our debriefing call.

My parents' experience highlights where disclosure falls short when it is the *only* strategy used to address the increasingly close ties between those caring for patients and the companies that sell the products used in the course of this care.

What is a patient to do with this information? When faced with an imminent major surgery and all its accompanying anxieties, not to mention the chronic pain, disrupted sleep, and physical limitations endured by someone who needs a new hip, patients are unlikely to be confident questioning their surgeon about these practices or to be in a position to evaluate whether the presence of the rep will compromise their care.[7]

How can disclosure really empower action if there is no alternative? As my dad's surgeon explained, all the orthopedic surgeons work with sales reps, which would preclude switching surgeons, and who would willingly exclude the so-called experts in a high-stakes situation? The unease, however, comes from wondering why the surgeon is not an "expert" in the use of the equipment or the implant he or she recommends. Or why an "expert" who provides advice on the implant also works on sales commission.

Without accompanying policies that place limits on interactions that lead to conflicts of interest and biased decision making, disclosures have the effect of making these kinds of relationships appear downright normal. The effect of the ubiquity of the gifts and payments from industry to physicians that the Sunshine Act has exposed is somewhat paralyzing: these relationships appear to be the status quo.[14] In reality, patients are rarely in a position to assess the impact of the relationship with industry, to seek an unconflicted second opinion, or to challenge their provider's advice.[7]

With disclosure happening at the level of the individual, we miss the bigger picture, in which sales representatives have become familiar fixtures in the clinical sphere and are often perceived as essential to the hospital's daily activities. Increasingly, hospitals rely on sales representatives to train clinicians in the use of products and equipment, to fund and conduct patient education, and to advise and support clinical procedures involving implants and complex devices. Although experts in their product, sales representatives generally do not have clinical training and should not be providing patient care or clinical recommendations.

The public has been excluded from taking part in the conversation about whether we want to outsource these clinical roles—patient teaching, clinician education, clinical advice—to for-profit entities that are driven by incentives that are misaligned with the aim of addressing the cost and quality crisis in healthcare.

Debunking Industry's Role in "Education"

The pharmaceutical and medical device industries have worked to position themselves as authorities in clinical practice in relation to their products. Sales representatives offered product training, and were available around the clock to provide product support. Sales reps have described this service package as a way they differentiate their product from those of their competitors.[3]

In this study, hospitals and clinicians welcomed the opportunity to outsource continuing and sometimes highly specialized education to the manufacturers of drugs and devices, recognizing sales representatives as product experts but also relying on them to fill resource gaps. While this outsourcing offered sales reps an opportunity to be in clinical spaces on a regular basis and to interact directly with clinicians, it also represented a growing service expectation, which may pressure industry representatives to work beyond their scope, for example, as a remedy to staff shortages.[15]

Outside of the hospital, nurses encountered industry-delivered education at trade shows, attended sponsored dinners accompanied by presentations from paid speakers, and invited industry representatives to present at or sponsor their professional meetings. As sales representatives increasingly took on training and support roles, health professionals and hospital administrators had a growing sense that industry was indispensable in the provision of care.

However, outsourcing these vital functions to industry has created a false economy. Nurse educators who reported relying on sales representatives to perform in-service education struggled to ensure that reps stayed on script, finding that reps frequently up-sold related devices or contradicted hospital policy, thus requiring that staff nurses be retrained. Sales reps providing support in the operating room or cardiac catheterization lab use these opportunities to promote high-cost products or introduce new products into practice, for which hospitals might receive unanticipated and sometimes large bills.[3] Those working in the purchasing departments explained that industry presentations at conferences were frequently the impetus for the landslide of new product requests that clinicians brought to purchasing committees, which struggled to verify the clinical need. On the other hand, clinical areas that seldom used expensive devices or equipment were rarely the recipients of industry-sponsored education, suggesting that industry provides this support only when it makes business sense and not on the basis of patient or staff needs.

The pharmaceutical industry has argued for the value of its marketing activities on the basis of their educational merit.[16] In response to growing scrutiny of their marketing activities, in the 2000s both the pharmaceutical and medical device trade associations released Codes of Conduct, which provide voluntary guidance for member companies.[17,18] Following a number of high-profile investigations and prosecutions into fraudulent marketing and billing practices by major drug companies under the Federal Anti-Kickback Statute in the late 1990s,[19] these industries needed to signal their willingness to self-regulate—which also served as a means to avoid stricter government oversight.[20,21]

These industry codes attempt to draw a line between relationships and gifts that are deemed "educational" and those that are "entertainment."[17,18] This distinction means that companies can provide "modest" meals in connection with presentations, or gifts of $100 or less that are "educational" in nature.[17] They also encourage industry support for continuing medical education, consulting arrangements, and company support for third-party educational or professional meetings.[17] The codes prohibit companies from providing entertainment or recreation, such as theater or sporting event tickets, golf, skiing or hunting trips, sporting equipment, or vacations.[17,18]

Though the industry has worked hard to distance itself from questionable sales tactics and to carve out a legitimate and credible role in healthcare, a growing body of research suggests the need to question the value of education provided by those with commercial interests.

Perhaps most tellingly, industry-sponsored "educational" events are rarely unaccompanied by food and other gifts. Uniquely in Australia, pharmaceutical companies were required to publicly report details of every sponsored event for health professionals.[4] From 2011 to 2015, companies sponsored, on average, more than 600 events per week.[22] Food and beverage were provided at more than 90% of these events, which included scientific meetings, journal clubs, clinical meetings, in-services, and grand rounds, ranging from a coffee cart to a sushi and fruit lunch to multicourse dinners with wine.[22] In the United States, payments in the form of food and drink are by far the most common type of payment: in 2015, of the approximately 72% of active physicians receiving some sort of payment from industry, 95% received food or beverage, at a median cost of $138 per person.[23] Indeed, there are few other educational contexts in which free food and drink are nearly guaranteed. This suggests that the true value of these events is not the information conveyed, but that sandwiches, coffees, and dinners out are a means to buy an audience with health professionals.

Nurses in this study also struggled with the bias inherent in the information that industry provided. Some acknowledged that the research sales reps gave them about products was skewed, particularly if the study had been funded or conducted by the manufacturer. In fact, if a drug or device study is sponsored by the product's manufacturer, it is significantly more likely to show that the product works and is safe compared to nonsponsored studies, even when the scientific methods are of equally high quality.[24] Others, who believed that the information provided had been carefully curated to present only the most favorable results, had to then go and do their own homework—a process that certainly didn't save any time.

In this way, a false knowledge economy has also developed. In providing training and support for their products, companies have little incentive to ensure that health professionals can use these products independently. They can thereby maintain an ongoing, dependent relationship between health professionals and product representatives, one in which these opportunities for interaction—and sales—remain frequent. Yet, believing that access to continuing education would be severely limited if industry were not to provide it freely, professional medical associations have fiercely defended industry-sponsored education, most recently introducing a bill to exclude education-related events from the Sunshine Act's reporting requirements.[25] However, it is patients and ultimately tax payers who shoulder the costs for overprescription, the rising costs of drugs and devices, and the side effects from products that are pushed to market too aggressively.

Addressing the Corporatization of Healthcare

In conducting this study, it was often difficult to identify the line between healthcare and industry. What began as an investigation into the interactions between nurses and industry representatives became an analysis of the commercialized situation in which most nurses in the United States work.

Sometimes nurses were employees of corporations. One hospital I visited was a subsidiary of a corporate national hospital chain, which operates its facilities for profit and is mandated to increase value for its shareholders. The nurses who worked at this hospital frequently grappled with the top-down decisions that were made about supplies and equipment, often on the basis of cost savings alone. Even the not-for-profit hospitals I visited had embraced corporate management models, adopting programs such as "lean methodology," pioneered by Toyota, employing consultants and managers to streamline hospital processes in the name of efficiency.

The drug and device industries were only two of many medically related industries that nurses encountered. Nurses at all four hospitals I visited pointed to the plethora of for-profit entities they regularly interacted with, ranging from health insurance companies, to staffing agencies, to private ambulance transport services, to the network of home care–related agencies that vied for their referrals. Just like the drug companies, the medics for the private ambulance service, for example, sometimes left a bountiful gift basket for the discharge nurses during the holiday season, and the break room refrigerator was peppered with promotional magnets for health-related services.

Interactions between health professionals and drug or device reps are certainly not the only source of tension between commercial interests and the safe, quality, and cost-effective care of patients. Corporations have appropriated increasing proportions of the health sector through mergers and acquisitions and the contracting out of services paid for with federal insurance.[6,26] The United States has ended up with the biggest and most expensive healthcare system in the world, though it lags behind other countries in terms of health outcomes.[6,27]

At heart, a tension exists between the legally mandated corporate mission to maximize profits for shareholders and the ethics underlying health professional practice.[28-30] Nurses have criticized the corporate model of healthcare delivery and the inequalities it has produced with its emphases on rationalization, efficiency, and profitability.[30-33] Nurses have described practicing in hospitals that adopted corporate models of efficiency, requiring that they ration their time and their care and operate under the assumption of scarce resources.[33] Here, continuing education, patient teaching, and the emotional aspects of care were most expendable.[33] Thus, in this study, when industry representatives offered resources that nurses otherwise couldn't access, this presented as an opportunity, not an ethical conflict. One nurse coordinated a bimonthly patient support group for people living with HIV/AIDs on behalf of a pharmaceutical sales rep who led the group in addition to bringing a hot lunch and gift cards to a grocery store. She resented the company's exploitation of a marketing opportunity but explained, "I can't deny my patients."[34]

When nurses discussed their relationships with for-profit industry, it was often with a similar sense of having little choice. The alternative to engaging industry seemed to be one in which patients were deprived of support services and nurses went without any product training or had to forgo conference attendance. More mundanely, nurses had relationships with industry at the behest of supervisors or as part of their routine job responsibilities.[34]

Relationships with sales reps were also only one set of interests that nurses had to contend with in caring for patients. Nursing has long been defined by the practice of balancing multiple, conflicting interests, characterized as "working in-between."[33,35-39] Freidson, a sociologist who studied the health professions, characterized the nurse as "the intense focus of conflicting perspectives" because the work of the nurse requires balancing individual patient needs and physician orders with the aggregate needs of the unit and the resources he or she has available.[37] This balancing act takes place within the context of staffing shortages, reduced lengths of stay for hospitalized patients, increasingly burdensome charting and reporting requirements, and frequent organizational restructuring.[32]

In "working in-between," however, nurses hold a significant balance of power in determining outcomes for patients and staff.[37] Nursing practice, in its commitment to face-to-face care, is also a site of resistance to the commodification of healthcare and technological development at any costs.[32] Thus, nurses are uniquely positioned to counter commercial influence within healthcare.

Registered nurses are situated differently from physicians within the healthcare system—both in the way their employment is structured and in their relationship to patients. For example, they typically are paid by the institutions in which they work, rather than by insurance or direct billing, and they rarely have economic interests that may be at risk with the adoption of new technologies, as might be true for a physician in a clinic. Nurses occupy the privileged position of belonging to the most trusted profession,[40] and they have the ethical and practical skill sets to manage conflicting interests that are essential in nursing work. However, to effectively address commercial influence in healthcare, nurses need to totally deconstruct the "as-if" myths around nursing practice and claim full recognition of the scope and importance of nurses' power and influence around treatment, purchasing, and administrative decision making.

Particularly, nurses have the ability to organize collectively and to challenge hospitals when decisions are made on the basis of finan-

cial priorities instead of what is best for patients. The nursing profession has a long history of advocating for social reform, which at
times has been eclipsed by apolitical or individually oriented models of bioethics.[39] As employees within the health system, nurses
are vulnerable to harmful repercussion from employers, and they
engage in advocacy often at great personal and professional risk.[39]
However, the nursing profession is one of the few unionized health
professions, which allows nurses to collectively advocate for safe
and quality care and to leverage the bargaining power of the largest group of health professionals. Unions, unlike professional associations, are independent of the medically related industry and hospitals and have the political power to challenge these interests in the
political arena.

For example, in 2006, Newton-Wellesley Hospital in Massachusetts introduced mandatory customer services scripts for nurses' interactions with patients at the recommendation of a marketing and
customer service consulting firm.[41] Adherence to these scripts was
to form the basis of nurses' professional evaluations. Because the
nurses were unionized, the hospital was required to negotiate with
the nurses before the policy could be fully implemented. The nurses
took action, educated their members, and negotiated instead for safe
staffing ratios and professional evaluations based on clinical compe-
tence and professional judgment as the basis for high-quality care.[41]
Wearing buttons proclaiming, "We are *not* Stepford Nurses," these
nurses asserted their loyalty to patients, not the institution, resisting
the corporatization of their practice.[41]

Decision making in healthcare happens collectively. Thus, we need
to challenge commercial influence over the healthcare environment
rather than its sway over individual clinicians. The environment in
which a professional works is the most significant influence over a professional's behavior, much more so than their education or professional
socialization.[37] Interactions with industry have become normal in clinical practice, and few clinicians see them as an ethical problem.[42-44]

Instead, we need to think about commercial interests as a systemic problem in healthcare and begin challenging the maxims of
the medical market that promote newer, expensive, long-term treat-

ments and amenities rather than cost-effective care or cure.[6] Challenging these market logics means that sales reps cannot be the authority when it comes to the safe or appropriate use of their own products and that health professionals need to be able to act independently of industry interests.

Policy Proposals

To address the pervasive influence of medically related industry in healthcare, it is necessary to institute real structural changes that include policy proposals to address the role of industry representatives in hospitals and their interactions with health professionals. It also means that health professionals from all disciplines should receive formal preparation for interacting with industry, particularly those taking on management or leadership roles. Addressing commercial influence within hospitals requires engaging bedside nurses as expert colleagues in policy discussions at the hospital, state, and national levels to design policies that are inclusive of nurses and relevant to nursing practice. Recognizing on the policy level what nurses really are doing, as opposed to what they are socially authorized to do, could help ensure that nursing expertise contributes to the development of better healthcare products and services in an ethical manner. Change could occur through reimbursement reform, the formation of nursing practice groups that are independent contractors of hospitals, or the revision of scope of practice to include at least the activities that nurses already perform.

I now propose a series of policy proposals that could help to build a climate that reduces the possibility of conflict of interest for individual health professionals, promotes transparency, and fosters ethical awareness in the context of interactions with industry. Medically related industry is an important part of healthcare—clinicians could not currently practice without the drugs, devices, equipment, and supplies produced by these companies. These proposals are designed to suggest ways to best work together: to promote developments in the quality and safety of care that are also cost-effective; to base decision making on unbiased information; to foster transparency and the preservation of public trust; and to prepare clinicians for this aspect of their practice.

Promoting Developments in the Quality and Safety of Care

Nurses should be encouraged to work with industry toward the design of better products. Many nurses work actively with industry to provide feedback on new and existing products, as do health professionals across disciplines. Capturing the perspectives of the people who use these products is essential if products are to be improved; nurses are also uniquely positioned to offer insight into patients' needs. Nurses' consulting work and participation in market research, however, should be disclosed to their employers and reported in Open Payments (under the Sunshine Act) if compensation is received, so that possible conflicts of interest can be evaluated and managed. Third-party market research that employs a double-blinded procedure (the company is not aware of the identity of the nurse consulting and the nurse is not aware of the product's brand) would be the best way to prevent conflicts of interest while allowing for collaboration.

Hospitals should create testing centers for staff nurses to trial products and provide feedback. Certain hospitals have created product-testing centers where staff nurses can handle and evaluate product samples independently of sales representatives. Nurses are seconded or volunteer to perform these evaluations, released from their normal work duties, and compensated for this time. In this setting, products can be compared head to head and evaluated systematically on criteria that are of value to nursing practice and hospital priorities. These test centers give nurses the opportunity to learn about products, ask questions, and provide feedback that can be shared with the administration, materials management, and manufacturers without the need for inducements and free from competing demands on nurses' attention.

Basing Decisions on Unbiased Information

Create a "Consumer Products Report" or a platform for crowd-sourced reviews for medical devices, equipment, and supplies. Nurses expressed the need for unbiased product information, particularly a means to compare products side by side. Purchasing committees relied on product references from other institutions or manufacturer-sponsored or -conducted studies, which sales representatives provided.[45] A not-for-profit organization, such as Consumer Reports (which accepts no advertising, pays for all products reviewed, and conducts its own testing), would be highly valuable to this sector in providing independent, unbiased reviews of medical products. Alternatively, hospitals could share and pool the results of their small-scale in-house product trials and product reviews in a web-based, crowd-sourced platform as a means to access product references directly.

Marketing, when inevitable, should be made as explicit and transparent as possible and occur in a group setting. Hospitals restrict sales representatives' access to decision makers and purchasing committees at varying levels. Some ban sales representatives from presenting to committees, preferring a setting in which clinicians speak directly to one another. While this kind of internal dialogue is important and serves to prevent fragmentation among clinicians, it also has the unintended consequence of requiring the "cold call" to occur outside of the formal, collective process and to establish it as an essential first step. Individuals are left to manage sales visits on their own time and are left susceptible to whatever marketing strategies are employed. The model of the "Farmer's Market," in which sales reps are invited to present to the committee as a whole might be a better model, because the marketing is explicit, and the committee collectively evaluates the information, mitigating the effects of individual clinician-industry relationships.

Researchers should develop tools to assist hospitals in making evidence-based evaluations of value. Due to the lack of available and unbiased evidence, making decisions about the value of medical devices and equipment is highly challenging for hospitals and purchasing committees.[46] Many hospital-based committees seeking to make decisions about cost-effectiveness and value lack explicit frameworks to support systematic and evidence-based decision making.[45,47] I propose a guiding framework to support purchasing committees attempting to evaluate products, devices, and equipment that could be applied across clinical specialties or product categories.[45] This framework prioritizes clinical and local expertise in establishing whether a product is needed, incorporates hospital-level data to understand how it will be used, and prompts a systematic, evidence-based evaluation of whether the product is superior to existing or competing products in terms of patient outcomes and, finally, cost.[45] Researchers could develop a similar framework targeted to the evaluation of products used in nursing care and based on outcomes of interest to nursing practice.

Fostering Transparency and Addressing Conflict of Interest

Industry relations and disclosure policies should be inclusive of all health professionals and staff. In the case of the Sunshine Act, all employees of institutions who receive reimbursement from Medicare or Medicaid should be subject to payment disclosures. Industry relations policies at the institutional level should also be inclusive of all disciplines and roles so that marketers cannot exploit loopholes or target clinicians differentially.

All institutions that receive federal reimbursement should also be subject to public disclosure of industry payments. Public disclosure of industry payments will make institutional conflicts of interest more transparent, allowing the analysis of patterns of sponsorship and the commercialization of healthcare environments.

Policies should prohibit clinicians from receiving gifts, including food and drink, from industry representatives. Disclosure is a critical, but limited first step toward addressing commercial influences;[7] however, disclosure does little to alter the conditions under which commercial influence occurs, and as a policy solution, leaves it to consumers who are in the weakest position to interpret and address these conditions.[48] If interactions with industry are indeed as beneficial and necessary as they are purported to be, clinicians should not require inducements in the form of gifts to participate.[49] This kind of approach would require the leadership not only of institutions but also of professional associations and licensing bodies, given that the boundaries of the workplace are highly permeable to the gifts that clinicians receive at conferences and other educational events.

Professional associations and licensing boards should require the disclosure of receipt of payments and prohibit the receipt of gifts. Upon recertification or license renewal, clinicians should report the receipt of payments, and this information should be made available to employers and the public and be subject to audit. While it may be difficult for institutions to effectively implement policies pertaining to activities outside of the workplace, the professional and licensing bodies to which clinicians are accountable may be important stakeholders in safeguarding professional judgment from marketing influence.

Realigning the Incentives

Industry representatives working in clinical spaces in a support capacity need clear role definition. A study of the experiences of industry-employed allied professionals, who regularly and directly interacted with patients while providing technical support for an implantable cardiac device, found that they experienced moral distress through role ambiguity.[15] They described the increasing burden of customer service expectations and the growth of inappropriate involvement, such as remedying staffing shortages and participating directly in patient care. They desired clearer role definition and boundaries to avoid being placed in compromising or distressing situations such as the deactivation of cardiac devices.[15] Similarly, in this study, the misalignment of incentives resulted in the blurring of boundaries between the support and sales aspects of the roles of industry support personnel. For example, the individual providing technical support in the operating room is frequently working on sales commission. In instances where industry provides essential expertise, this expertise should be compensated, rather than its cost passed on to the patient or insurer. This compensation will make more transparent the value of industry expertise and the costs of providing this kind of service, and perhaps foster the more effective use of hospital human resources.

Optimally, hospitals should invest in experts who can provide product support in-house. Clinical nurse specialists and biomedical engineers are just two groups of experts who could provide continuing education, product evaluation, and product support in-house. Hospitals have set a precedent for this model of expertise for certain clinical conditions, such as sepsis, by hiring nurse specialists to conduct coordinated efforts hospital-wide.[50] Although human resources are costly, these experts can enable hospitals to offer a selection of devices and products that are cost-effective and that clinicians can safely, and independently, use in the service of better patient outcomes.

Preparing Clinicians for Interacting with Industry

Interacting with industry should be included in the preparation of health professionals, and especially nurse managers and leaders. Although interacting with industry is commonplace for many health professionals, most lack preparation in their formal education, workplace orientation, and ongoing continuing education for this aspect of their role. In particular, the development of critical appraisal skills necessary to adequately research new products for purchase and to evaluate research, and education content is paramount.[51] In this study, nurses admitted that they had never had occasion to discuss interacting with industry, the challenges and benefits, or the ethical issues that arose in their professional lives. Health professionals need ethics education that is grounded in practice and actively confronts the gap between the ideal and the real. Having an ethical framework grounded in practice may be more empowering than content addressing generic ethical principles or concepts, such as conflict of interest, which often seem remote from daily experiences.[52] It may also allow health professionals to more clearly articulate their ambivalence and to identify ethical situations as they arise.[52]

Preserving Trust

When I have spoken of my findings to family, friends, or other members of the lay public, most admitted that they had no knowledge of the degree to which sales representatives were built into the day-to-day functioning of hospitals, and yet they expressed a deep concern over reports that sales representatives were frequently present in clinical spaces. In order to preserve the public's trust in the healthcare system and to work toward advances that will improve the safety, quality, and cost of healthcare, the health sector needs to adopt policies that ensure transparency, address bias in education and research, align incentives to stem commercial influence, and foster an ethical climate that prioritizes the public interest.

Nurses in this study were not typically the recipients of large payments, trips to Hawaii, personal gifts, or patent royalties—unlike the physicians sometimes profiled in the media—although participants reported that nurse colleagues were sometimes the recipients of such gifts. Instead, nurses described how industry representatives and their product information and marketing activities were so much a part of their everyday practice that they were largely taken for granted. Interacting with industry was frequently built into nurses' job descriptions, as a part of routine patient care or a source of information needed for their practice. Industry was also the source of samples, lavish dinners, the spectacle that was the annual trade show, and free lunches. Although many participants attempted to create a boundary between marketing activities and the service, support, and information functions that industry fulfilled, nurses also described how these things frequently traveled together. It was sometimes difficult to separate the service from the sales; at other times, the sales function was tolerated due to the need for the service.

Nurses—held high in the public's esteem and expertly positioned to act as patient advocates—may be the clinicians most able to mitigate the harms of commercial interests in clinical practice. This ability will require that the relationships between clinicians, healthcare institutions, and medically related industry be made visible, that concerns about these relationships be made audible, and that the work of taking care of others be valued.

REFERENCES

Chapter 1. Invisible Influence

1. Charles Ornstein and Ryann Grochowski Jones. "A Pharma Payment a Day Keeps Docs' Finances Okay." *ProPublica*, July 1, 2015, https://www.propublica.org/article/a-pharma-payment-a-day-keeps-docs-finances-ok.
2. Centers for Medicare & Medicaid Services. "Medicare, Medicaid, Children's Health Insurance Programs: Transparency Reports and Reporting of Physician Ownership or Investment Interests." Centers for Medicare & Medicaid Services. *Federal Register* 78, no. 27 (2013): 9458–528.
3. Centers for Medicare & Medicaid Services. "The Facts about Open Payments Data." Centers for Medicare & Medicaid Services, accessed March 9, 2018, https://openpaymentsdata.cms.gov/summary.
4. Gardiner Harris, Benedict Carey, and Janet Roberts. "Psychiatrists, Troubled Children, and the Drug Industry's Role." *New York Times*, May 10, 2007, A1.
5. Paul D. Thacker. "The Slow Pace of Success in a 'Do Something Congress.'" *Edmond J. Safra Center for Ethics Blog,* February 20, 2013, https://ethics.harvard.edu/blog/slow-pace-success-do-something-congress.
6. Charles Grassley. "Grassley, Kohl Say Public Should Know When Pharmaceutical Makers Give Money to Doctors." Press release, September 6, 2007, http://www.grassley.senate.gov/news/news-releases/grassley-kohl-say-public-should-know-when-pharmaceutical-makers-give-money.
7. Shantanu Agrawal and Douglas Brown. "The Physician Payments Sunshine Act—Two Years of the Open Payments Program." *New England Journal of Medicine* 374, no. 10 (2016): 906–9.
8. Colleen DeJong, Thomas Aguilar, Chien-Wen Tseng, Grace A. Lin, W. John Boscardin, and R. Adams Dudley. "Pharmaceutical Industry–Sponsored Meals and Physician Prescribing Patterns for Medicare Beneficiaries." *JAMA Internal Medicine* 176, no. 8 (2016): 1114–22.
9. James S. Yeh, Jessica M. Franklin, Jerry Avorn, Joan Landon, and Aaron S. Kesselheim. "Association of Industry Payments to Physicians with the Prescribing of Brand-Name Statins in Massachusetts." *JAMA Internal Medicine* 176, no. 6 (2016): 763–68.
10. William Fleischman, Shantanu Agrawal, Marissa King, Arjun K. Venkatesh, Harlan M. Krumholz, Douglas McKee, Douglas Brown, and

Joseph S. Ross. "Association between Payments from Manufacturers of Pharmaceuticals to Physicians and Regional Prescribing: Cross Sectional Ecological Study." *British Medical Journal* 354 (2016): i4189.

11. Charles Ornstein, Ryann Grochowski Jones, and Mike Tigas. "Now There's Proof: Docs Who Get Company Cash Tend to Prescribe More Brand-Name Meds." *ProPublica*, March 17, 2016, https://www.propublica.org/article/doctors-who-take-company-cash-tend-to-prescribe-more-brand-name-drugs.

12. Karen E. Lasser, Paul D. Allen, Steffie J. Woolhandler, David U. Himmelstein, Sidney M. Wolfe, and David H. Bor. "Timing of New Black Box Warnings and Withdrawals for Prescription Medications." *Journal of the American Medical Association* 287, no. 17 (2002): 2215-20.

13. M. Angell. *The Truth about the Drug Companies: How They Deceive Us and What to Do about It*. New York: Random House, 2005.

14. IMS Health. *Global Pharmaceuticals Marketing Channel Reference*. Paris: IMS Health, 2015.

15. Marc-Andre Gagnon and Joel Lexchin. "The Cost of Pushing Pills: A New Estimate of Pharmaceutical Promotion Expenditures in the United States." *PLoS Medicine* 5, no. 1 (2008): e1.

16. Britta L. Anderson, Gabriel K. Silverman, George F. Loewenstein, Stanley Zinberg, and Jay Schulkin. "Factors Associated with Physicians' Reliance on Pharmaceutical Sales Representatives." *Academic Medicine* 84, no. 8 (2009): 994-1002.

17. Jason Hall, Judith Cantrill, and Peter Noyce. "Professional Issues: The Information Sources Used by Community Nurse Prescribers." *British Journal of Nursing* 12, no. 13 (2003): 810-18.

18. William H. Shrank, Joshua N. Liberman, Michael A. Fischer, Charmaine Girdish, Troyen A. Brennan, and Niteesh K. Choudhry. "Physician Perceptions about Generic Drugs." *Annals of Pharmacotherapy* 45, no. 1 (2011): 31-38.

19. Barbara Mintzes, Joel Lexchin, Jason M. Sutherland, Marie-Dominique Beaulieu, Michael S. Wilkes, Geneviève Durrieu, and Ellen Reynolds. "Pharmaceutical Sales Representatives and Patient Safety: A Comparative Prospective Study of Information Quality in Canada, France, and the United States." *Journal of General Internal Medicine* 28, no. 10 (2013): 1368-75.

20. Kalman Applbaum. "Getting to Yes: Corporate Power and the Creation of a Psychopharmaceutical Blockbuster." *Culture, Medicine, and Psychiatry* 33, no. 2 (2009): 185-215.

21. Aaron S. Kesselheim, Michelle M. Mello, and David M. Studdert. "Strategies and Practices in Off-Label Marketing of Pharmaceuticals: A Retrospective Analysis of Whistleblower Complaints." *PLoS Medicine* 8, no. 4 (2011): e1000431.

22. Michael A. Steinman, Lisa A. Bero, Mary-Margaret Chren, and Seth C. Landefeld. "Narrative Review: The Promotion of Gabapentin—an Analysis of Internal Industry Documents." *Annals of Internal Medicine* 145, no. 4 (2006): 284–93.

23. Josh Katz. "Drug Deaths in America Are Rising Faster Than Ever." *New York Times*, June 5, 2017.

24. Anna Lembke. *Drug Dealer, MD: How Doctors Were Duped, Patients Got Hooked, and Why It's So Hard to Stop*. Baltimore: Johns Hopkins University Press, 2016.

25. Quinn Grundy. "The Physician Payments Sunshine Act and the Unaddressed Role of Nurses: An Interest Group Analysis." *Policy, Politics & Nursing Practice* 13, no. 3 (2012): 154–61.

26. Quinn Grundy, Lisa Bero, and Ruth Malone. "Interactions between Non-physician Clinicians and Industry: A Systematic Review." *PLoS Medicine* 10, no. 11 (2013): e1001561.

27. Charles Ornstein. "Bill Would Add Nurses, Physician Assistants to Pharma Payments Database." *ProPublica*, October 8, 2015, http://www.propublica.org/article/bill-would-add-nurses-physician-assistants-to-pharma-payments-database.

28. There were 8,506,740 healthcare professionals in the United States in 2017, and 2,906,840 of these were registered nurses. Bureau of Labor Statistics. "Occupational Employment Statistics." United States Department of Labor, https://www.bls.gov/oes/current/oes_stru.htm#29-0000.

29. Quinn Grundy, Alice Fabbri, Barbara Mintzes, Swestika Swandari, and Lisa A. Bero. "The Inclusion of Nurses in Pharmaceutical Industry-Sponsored Events: Guess Who Is Also Coming to Dinner?" *JAMA Internal Medicine* 176, no. 11 (2016): 1718–20.

30. Scott Stump. "Watch Miss America Contestant's Heartwarming Monologue about Being a Nurse." *Today*, September 12, 2015, https://www.today.com/style/watch-miss-america-contestants-heartwarming-monologue-about-being-nurse-t43571.

31. Aurelie Corinthios. "Miss Colorado Kelley Johnson Defends Nurse Monologue after Being Mocked on *The View*." *People*, September 17, 2015, http://people.com/tv/miss-colorado-defends-nurse-monologue-after-joy-behar-mocked-her-on-the-view/.

32. Institute of Medicine. *The Future of Nursing: Leading Change, Advancing Health*. Washington, DC: Institute of Medicine, 2011.

33. Annemarie Jutel and David B. Menkes. "Soft Targets: Nurses and the Pharmaceutical Industry." *PLoS Medicine* 5, no. 2 (2008): e5.

34. Annemarie Jutel and David B. Menkes. "Nurses' Reported Influence on the Prescription and Use of Medication." *International Nursing Review* 57, no. 1 (2010): 92–97.

35. Joe Dumit. *Drugs for Life: How Pharmaceutical Companies Define Our Health*. Durham, NC: Duke University Press, 2012.
36. Kathleen E. McKone-Sweet, Paul Hamilton, and Susan B. Willis. "The Ailing Healthcare Supply Chain: A Prescription for Change." *Journal of Supply Chain Management* 41, no. 1 (2005): 4-17.
37. Quinn Grundy. "'Whether Something Cool Is Good Enough': The Role of Evidence, Sales Representatives, and Nurses' Expertise in Hospital Purchasing Decisions." *Social Science & Medicine* 165 (2016): 82-91.
38. Susan Chimonas, Susanna D. Evarts, Sarah K. Littlehale, and David J. Rothman. "Managing Conflicts of Interest in Clinical Care: The 'Race to the Middle' at U.S. Medical Schools." *Academic Medicine* 88, no.10 (2013): 1464-70.
39. Megan Brenan. "Nurses Keep Healthy Lead as Most Honest, Ethical Profession." Gallup, December 26, 2017, http://news.gallup.com/poll/224639 /nurses-keep-healthy-lead-honest-ethical-profession.aspx.

Chapter 2. From Sales to Service

1. Kalman Applbaum. "Getting to Yes: Corporate Power and the Creation of a Psychopharmaceutical Blockbuster." *Culture, Medicine, and Psychiatry* 33, no. 2 (2009): 185-215.
2. Rebecca Vesely. "Managing Points of Access." *Health Facilities Management* 26, no. 10 (2013): 39-46.
3. Joint Commission. "Identification Badge Requirements." Joint Commission, October 23, 2015, http://www.jointcommission.org/mobile/standards _information/jcfaqdetails.aspx?StandardsFAQId=99&StandardsFAQ ChapterId=64.
4. VCS. "Vendor Credentialing Service." July 7, 2011, https://vcsdatabase .com/vcs.php.
5. Otho Boone. "Don't Let Common Sense Take a Back Seat to Technology." *Biomedical Instrumentation and Technology* 43, no. 5 (2009): 346-47.
6. Quinn Grundy. "'Whether Something Cool Is Good Enough': The Role of Evidence, Sales Representatives and Nurses' Expertise in Hospital Purchasing Decisions." *Social Science & Medicine* 165 (2016): 82-91.
7. Robert Hodgson, Richard Allen, Ellen Broderick, J. Martin Bland, Jo C. Dumville, Rebecca Ashby, Sally Bell-Syer, et al. "Funding Source and the Quality of Reports of Chronic Wounds Trials: 2004 to 2011." *Trials* 15 (2014): 19.
8. Andreas Lundh, Joel Lexchin, Barbara Mintzes, Jeppe B. Schroll, and Lisa Bero. "Industry Sponsorship and Research Outcome." *Cochrane Database of Systematic Reviews*, no. 2 (2017): MR000033.
9. US Food and Drug Administration. "Medical Gowns." US Food and Drug Administration, accessed August 30, 2017, https://www.fda.gov/Medical

Devices/ProductsandMedicalProcedures/GeneralHospitalDevicesand
Supplies/PersonalProtectiveEquipment/ucm452775.htm.

10. Barbara Mintzes, Swestika Swandari, Alice Fabbri, Quinn Grundy, Ray
Moynihan, and Lisa Bero. "Does Industry-Sponsored Education Foster
Overdiagnosis and Overtreatment of Depression, Osteoporosis and Over-
active Bladder Syndrome? An Australian Cohort Study." *BMJ Open*, no. 8
(2018): e019027.

11. Quinn Grundy. "'My Love-Hate Relationship': Ethical Issues Associated
with Nurses' Interactions with Industry." *Nursing Ethics* 21, no. 5 (2013):
554-64.

12. Annemarie Jutel and David B. Menkes. "Soft Targets: Nurses and the
Pharmaceutical Industry." *PLoS Medicine* 5, no. 2 (2008): e5.

Chapter 3. "The Perfect Friend"

1. Karen B. Lasater. "Invisible Economics of Nursing: Analysis of a Hospital
Bill through a Foucauldian Perspective." *Nursing Philosophy* 15, no. 3
(2014): 221-24.

2. Kalman Applbaum. "Getting to Yes: Corporate Power and the Creation
of a Psychopharmaceutical Blockbuster." *Culture, Medicine, and Psychiatry*
33, no. 2 (2009): 185-215.

3. R. Anne Springer. "Pharmaceutical Industry Discursives and the Marketi-
zation of Nursing Work: A Case Example." *Nursing Philosophy* 12, no. 3
(2011): 214-28.

4. Megan Brenan. "Nurses Keep Healthy Lead as Most Honest, Ethical Profession." Gallup, December 26, 2017, http://news.gallup.com/poll/224639
/nurses-keep-healthy-lead-honest-ethical-profession.aspx.

5. Quinn Grundy. "'My Love-Hate Relationship': Ethical Issues Associated
with Nurses' Interactions with Industry." *Nursing Ethics* 21, no. 5 (2013):
554-64.

6. Michael Oldani. "Thick Prescriptions: Toward an Interpretation of Pharmaceutical Sales Practices." *Medical Anthropology Quarterly* 18, no. 3 (2004):
325-56.

7. Adriane Fugh-Berman and Shahram Ahari. "Following the Script: How
Drug Reps Make Friends and Influence Doctors." *PLoS Medicine* 4, no. 4
(2007): e150.

8. Dana Katz, Arthur L. Caplan, and Jon F. Merz. "All Gifts Large and Small:
Toward an Understanding of the Ethics of Pharmaceutical Industry Gift
Giving." *American Journal of Bioethics* 10, no. 10 (2010): 11-17.

9. Paul M. McNeill, Ian H. Kerridge, David A. Henry, Barrie Stokes, S. R. Hill,
David Newby, G. J. Macdonald, et al. "Giving and Receiving of Gifts
between Pharmaceutical Companies and Medical Specialists in Australia."
Internal Medicine Journal 36, no. 9 (2006): 571-78.

10. Ashley Wazana. "Physicians and the Pharmaceutical Industry: Is a Gift Ever Just a Gift?" *Journal of the American Medical Association* 283, no. 3 (2000): 373-80.

11. Paul S. Mueller, Abigale L. Ottenberg, David L. Hayes, and Barbara A. Koenig. "'I Felt Like the Angel of Death': Role Conflicts and Moral Distress among Allied Professionals Employed by the US Cardiovascular Implantable Electronic Device Industry." *Journal of Interventional Cardiology and Electrophysiology* 32, no. 3 (2011): 253-61.

12. Sergio Sismondo. "How to Make Opinion Leaders and Influence People." *Canadian Medical Association Journal* 187, no. 10 (2015): 759-60.

13. David J. Rothman and Susan Chimonas. "Academic Medical Centers' Conflict of Interest Policies." *Journal of the American Medical Association* 304, no. 20 (2010): 2294-95.

14. Susan Chimonas, M. DiLorenzo, and David J. Rothman. "Paradigms of Change: Case Studies in Transforming Physician-Industry Interactions." *Journal of Entrepreneurship and Organisation Management* 5, no. 3 (2016): 1000195.

15. Pharmaceutical Research and Manufacturers of America. *Code on Interactions with Healthcare Professionals*. Washington, DC: PhRMA, 2009.

Chapter 4. The "As-If" World of Nursing Practice

1. Colleen DeJong, Thomas Aguilar, Chien-Wen Tseng, Grace A. Lin, W. John Boscardin, and R. Adams Dudley. "Pharmaceutical Industry-Sponsored Meals and Physician Prescribing Patterns for Medicare Beneficiaries." *JAMA Internal Medicine* 176, no. 8 (2016): 1114-22.

2. James S. Yeh, Jessica M. Franklin, Jerry Avorn, Joan Landon, and Aaron S. Kesselheim. "Association of Industry Payments to Physicians with the Prescribing of Brand-Name Statins in Massachusetts." *JAMA Internal Medicine* 176, no. 6 (2016): 763-68.

3. William Fleischman, Shantanu Agrawal, Marissa King, Arjun K. Venkatesh, Harlan M. Krumholz, Douglas McKee, Douglas Brown, et al. "Association between Payments from Manufacturers of Pharmaceuticals to Physicians and Regional Prescribing: Cross Sectional Ecological Study." *British Medical Journal* 354 (2016): i4189.

4. Joint Commission. "National Patient Safety Goals Effective January 2018: Hospital Accreditation Program." Joint Commission, accessed March 13, 2018, https://www.jointcommission.org/assets/1/6/NPSG_Chapter_HAP_Jan2018.pdf.

5. Karen B. Lasater. "Invisible Economics of Nursing: Analysis of a Hospital Bill through a Foucauldian Perspective." *Nursing Philosophy* 15, no. 3 (2014): 221-24.

6. John M. Welton, Laurie Zone-Smith, and Mary H. Fischer. "Adjustment of Inpatient Care Reimbursement for Nursing Intensity." *Policy, Politics & Nursing Practice* 7, no. 4 (2006): 270–80.

7. Eliot Freidson. *Profession of Medicine: A Study of the Sociology of Applied Knowledge*. Chicago: University of Chicago Press, 1970.

8. Susan Reverby. *Ordered to Care: The Dilemma of American Nursing, 1850–1945*. Cambridge: Cambridge University Press, 1987.

9. Paul Starr. *The Social Transformation of American Medicine*. New York: Basic Books, 1984.

10. American Nurses Association. *Code of Ethics for Nurses with Interpretive Statements*. Silver Spring, MD: American Nurses Association, 2015.

11. American Nurses Association. *Code of Ethics for Nurses*. Silver Spring, MD: American Nurses Association, 2001.

12. Suzanne Gordon. *Nursing against the Odds: How Health Care Cost Cutting, Media Stereotypes, and Medical Hubris Undermine Nurses and Patient Care*. Ithaca, NY: Cornell University Press, 2005.

13. Annemarie Jutel and David B. Menkes. "'But Doctors Do It . . . ': Nurses' Views of Gifts and Information from the Pharmaceutical Industry." *Annals of Pharmacotherapy* 43, no. 6 (2009): 1057–63.

Chapter 5. "There Are Rules of Engagement"

1. Quinn Grundy "'My Love-Hate Relationship': Ethical Issues Associated with Nurses' Interactions with Industry." *Nursing Ethics* 21, no. 5 (2013): 554–64.

2. Arne J. Vetlesen. *Perception, Empathy, and Judgment: An Inquiry into the Preconditions of Moral Performance*. Philadelphia: Pennsylvania State University Press, 1994.

3. Eloise B. Cathcart, Miriam Greenspan, and Matthew Quin. "The Making of a Nurse Manager: The Role of Experiential Learning in Leadership Development." *Journal of Nursing Management* 18, no. 4 (2010): 330–47.

4. Megan Brenan. "Nurses Keep Healthy Lead as Most Honest, Ethical Profession." Gallup, December 26, 2017, http://news.gallup.com/poll/224639 /nurses-keep-healthy-lead-honest-ethical-profession.aspx.

5. Centers for Disease Control and Prevention. "Sepsis." Centers for Disease Control and Prevention, September 16, 2016, https://www.cdc.gov/sepsis /index.html.

6. Adriane Fugh-Berman and Shahram Ahari. "Following the Script: How Drug Reps Make Friends and Influence Doctors." *PLoS Medicine* 4, no. 4 (2007): e150.

7. Deborah Korenstein, Salomeh Keyhani, and Joseph S. Ross. "Physician Attitudes toward Industry: A View across the Specialties." *Archives of Surgery* 145, no. 6 (2010): 570–77.

8. Quinn Grundy, Lisa Bero, and Ruth Malone. "Interactions between Non-physician Clinicians and Industry: A Systematic Review." *PLoS Medicine* 10, no. 11 (2013): e1001561.

9. Melissa A. Fischer, Mary E. Keough, Joann L. Baril, Laura Saccoccio, Kathleen M. Mazor, Elissa Ladd, Ann Von Worley, et al. "Prescribers and Pharmaceutical Representatives: Why Are We Still Meeting?" *Journal of General Internal Medicine* 24, no. 7 (2009): 795-801.

10. Susan Chimonas, Troyen A. Brennan, and David J. Rothman. "Physicians and Drug Representatives: Exploring the Dynamics of the Relationship." *Journal of General Internal Medicine* 22, no. 2 (2007): 184-90.

11. Michael Oldani. "Thick Prescriptions: Toward an Interpretation of Pharmaceutical Sales Practices." *Medical Anthropology Quarterly* 18, no. 3 (2004): 325-56.

12. Dana Katz, Arthur L. Caplan, and John F. Merz. "All Gifts Large and Small: Toward an Understanding of the Ethics of Pharmaceutical Industry Gift Giving." *American Journal of Bioethics* 10, no. (2010): 11-17.

13. Christopher Mayes, Jane Williams, Ian Kerridge, and Wendy Lipworth. "Scientism, Conflicts of Interest, and the Marginalization of Ethics in Medical Education." *Journal of Evaluation in Clinical Practice* (2017): doi.10.1111/jep.12843.

14. Ian Larkin, Desmond Ang, Jonathan Steinhart, Matthew Chau, Mark Patterson, Sunita Sah, Tina Wu, et al. "Association between Academic Medical Center Pharmaceutical Detailing Policies and Physician Prescribing." *Journal of the American Medical Association* 317, no. 17 (2017): 1785-95.

15. Sarah Wadmann. "Physician-Industry Collaboration: Conflicts of Interest and the Imputation of Motive." *Social Studies of Science* 44, no. 4 (2014): 531-54.

16. American Nurses Association. *Code of Ethics for Nurses with Interpretive Statements.* Silver Spring, MD: American Nurses Association, 2015.

Chapter 6. Marketing to Nurses Matters

1. Kalman Applbaum. "Getting to Yes: Corporate Power and the Creation of a Psychopharmaceutical Blockbuster." *Culture, Medicine, and Psychiatry* 33, no. 2 (2009): 185-215.

2. Quinn Grundy, Alice Fabbri, Barbara Mintzes, Swestika Swandari, and Lisa A. Bero. "The Inclusion of Nurses in Pharmaceutical Industry-Sponsored Events: Guess Who Is Also Coming to Dinner?" *JAMA Internal Medicine* 176, no. 11 (2016): 1718-20.

3. Bonnie O'Connor, Fran Pollner, and Adriane Fugh-Berman. "Salespeople in the Surgical Suite: Relationships between Surgeons and Medical Device Representatives." *PLoS One* 11, no. 8 (2016): e0158510.

4. Jane Robertson, Ray Moynihan, Emily Walkom, Lisa Bero, and David

Henry. "Mandatory Disclosure of Pharmaceutical Industry-Funded Events for Health Professionals." *PLoS Medicine* 6, no. 11 (2009): e1000128.

5. Ancella Santos. *The Sun Shines on Europe: Transparency of Financial Relationships in the Healthcare Sector*. Amsterdam: Health Action International, 2017.

6. Elizabeth Rosenthal. *An American Sickness: How Healthcare Became Big Business and How You Can Take It Back*. New York: Penguin Press, 2017.

7. Sunita Sah. "Conflicts of Interest and Your Physician: Psychological Processes That Cause Unexpected Changes in Behavior." *Journal of Law Medicine and Ethics* 40, no. 3 (2012): 482–87.

8. Institute of Medicine. *Conflict of Interest in Medical Research, Education, and Practice*. Washington, DC: National Academies Press, 2009.

9. Charles Grassley. "Grassley, Kohl Say Public Should Know When Pharmaceutical Makers Give Money to Doctors." Press release, September 6, 2007, http://www.grassley.senate.gov/news/news-releases/grassley-kohl-say-public-should-know-when-pharmaceutical-makers-give-money.

10. Centers for Medicare & Medicaid Services. "Open Payments Data in Context." Department of Health & Human Services, accessed August 31, 2017, https://www.cms.gov/OpenPayments/About/Open-Payments-Data-in-Context.html.

11. Alison R. Hwong, Sunita Sah, and Lisa Soleymani Lehmann. "The Effects of Public Disclosure of Industry Payments to Physicians on Patient Trust: A Randomized Experiment." *Journal of General Internal Medicine* (2017): doi:10.1007/s11606-017-4122-y.

12. George Loewenstein, Sunita Sah, and Daylian M. Cain. "The Unintended Consequences of Conflict of Interest Disclosure." *Journal of the American Medical Association* 307, no. 7 (2012): 669–70.

13. Sunita Sah, George Loewenstein, and Daylian M. Cain. "The Burden of Disclosure: Increased Compliance with Distrusted Advice." *Journal of Personality and Social Psychology* 104, no. 2 (2013): 289–304.

14. Charles Ornstein and Ryann Grochowski Jones. "A Pharma Payment a Day Keeps Docs' Finances Okay." *ProPublica*, July 1, 2015, https://www.propublica.org/article/a-pharma-payment-a-day-keeps-docs-finances-ok.

15. Paul S. Mueller, Abigale L. Ottenberg, David L. Hayes, and Barbara A. Koenig. "'I Felt Like the Angel of Death': Role Conflicts and Moral Distress among Allied Professionals Employed by the US Cardiovascular Implantable Electronic Device Industry." *Journal of Interventional Cardiology and Electrophysiology* 32, no. 3 (2011): 253–61.

16. Pharmaceutical Research and Manufacturers of America. *Pharmaceutical Marketing in Perspective: Its Value and Role as One of Many Factors Informing Prescribing*. Washington, DC: PhRMA, 2008.

17. Pharmaceutical Research and Manufacturers of America. *Code on Interactions with Healthcare Professionals*. Washington, DC: PhRMA, 2009.

18. Advanced Medical Technology Association. *Code of Ethics on Interactions with Health Care Professionals.* Washington, DC: AdvaMed, 2009.

19. Susan Chimonas and David J. Rothman. "New Federal Guidelines for Physician-Pharmaceutical Industry Relations: The Politics of Policy Formation." *Health Affairs* 24, no. 4 (2005): 949–60.

20. Thomas P. Lyon and John W. Maxwell. "Astroturf: Interest Group Lobbying and Corporate Strategy." *Journal of Economics and Management Strategy* 13, no. 4 (2004): 561–97.

21. Quinn Grundy. "The Physician Payments Sunshine Act and the Unaddressed Role of Nurses: An Interest Group Analysis." *Policy, Politics & Nursing Practice* 13, no. 3 (2012): 154–61.

22. Alice Fabbri, Quinn Grundy, Barbara Mintzes, Swestika Swandari, Ray Moynihan, Emily Walkom, and Lisa A. Bero. "A Cross-Sectional Analysis of Pharmaceutical Industry–Funded Events for Health Professionals in Australia." *BMJ Open* 7, no. 6 (2017).

23. Robert Steinbrook. "Physicians, Industry Payments for Food and Beverages, and Drug Prescribing." *Journal of the American Medical Association* 317, no. 17 (2017): 1753–54.

24. Andreas Lundh, Joel Lexchin, Barbara Mintzes, Jeppe B. Schroll, and Lisa Bero. "Industry Sponsorship and Research Outcome." *Cochrane Database of Systematic Reviews*, no. 2 (2017): MR000033.

25. Ed Silverman. "Medical Groups Push to Water Down Requirements for Disclosing Industry Ties." *STAT News*, July 21, 2016, https://www.stat news.com/pharmalot/2016/07/21/ama-cms-payments-to-doctors/.

26. Adele E. Clarke, Laura Mamo, Jennifer R. Fishman, Janet K. Shim, and Jennifer R. Fosket. "Biomedicalization: Technoscientific Transformations of Health, Illness, and U.S. Biomedicine." *American Sociological Review* 68 (2003): 161–94.

27. Karen Davis, Kristof Stremikis, David Squires, and Cathy Schoen. "Mirror, Mirror on the Wall: How the Performance of the U.S. Health Care System Compares Internationally." Commonwealth Fund, 2014, accessed August 31, 2017, http://www.commonwealthfund.org/publications/fund -reports/2014/jun/mirror-mirror.

28. Betty Bekemeier and Patricia Butterfield. "Unreconciled Inconsistencies: A Critical Review of the Concept of Social Justice in Three National Nursing Documents." *Advances in Nursing Science* 28, no. 2 (2005): 152–62.

29. Adeline Falk-Rafael. "Speaking Truth to Power: Nursing's Legacy and Moral Imperative." *Advances in Nursing Science* 28, no. 3 (2005): 212–23.

30. Carol Schroeder. "The Tyranny of Profit: Concentration of Wealth, Corporate Globalization, and the Failed US Health Care System." *Advances in Nursing Science* 26, no. 3 (2003): 173–84.

31. Wendy J. Austin. "The Incommensurability of Nursing as a Practice and

the Customer Service Model: An Evolutionary Threat to the Discipline." *Nursing Philosophy* 12, no. 3 (2011): 158-66.

32. Ruth E. Malone. "Distal Nursing." *Social Science & Medicine* 56, no. 11 (2003): 2317-26.

33. Colleen Varcoe, Gweneth Doane, Bernadette Pauly, Paddy Rodney, Janet L. Storch, Karen Mahoney, Gladys McPherson, et al. "Ethical Practice in Nursing: Working the In-Betweens." *Journal of Advanced Nursing* 45, no. 3 (2004): 316-25.

34. Quinn Grundy. "'My Love-Hate Relationship': Ethical Issues Associated with Nurses' Interactions with Industry." *Nursing Ethics* 21, no. 5 (2013): 554-64.

35. Anne H. Bishop and John R. Scudder Jr. *The Practical, Moral, and Personal Sense of Nursing: A Phenomenological Philosophy of Practice*. Albany: State University of New York Press, 1990.

36. Patricia D'Antonio. *American Nursing: A History of Knowledge, Authority, and the Meaning of Work*. Baltimore: Johns Hopkins University Press, 2010.

37. Eliot Freidson. *Profession of Medicine: A Study of the Sociology of Applied Knowledge*. Chicago: University of Chicago Press, 1970.

38. Susan Reverby. *Ordered to Care: The Dilemma of American Nursing, 1850-1945*. Cambridge: Cambridge University Press, 1987.

39. Roland R. Yarling and Beverly J. McElmurry. "The Moral Foundation of Nursing." *Advances in Nursing Science* 8, no. 2 (1986): 63-73.

40. Megan Brenan. "Nurses Keep Healthy Lead as Most Honest, Ethical Profession." Gallup, December 26, 2017, http://news.gallup.com/poll/224639/nurses-keep-healthy-lead-honest-ethical-profession.aspx.

41. Massachusetts Nurses Association. "Newton-Wellesley RNs Oppose Wal-Martization of Nursing Practice." *Massachusetts Nurse* 77, no. 3 (2006): 1, 13.

42. Deborah Korenstein, Salomeh Keyhani, and Joseph S. Ross. "Physician Attitudes toward Industry: A View across the Specialties." *Archives of Surgery* 145, no. 6 (2010): 570-77.

43. Nancy Crigger, Kirsten Barnes, Autumn Junko, Sarah Rahal, and Casey Sheek. "Nurse Practitioners' Perceptions and Participation in Pharmaceutical Marketing." *Journal of Advanced Nursing* 65, no. 3 (2009): 525-33.

44. Annemarie Jutel and David B. Menkes, "'But Doctors Do It . . .': Nurses' Views of Gifts and Information from the Pharmaceutical Industry." *Annals of Pharmacotherapy* 43, no. 6 (2009): 1057-63.

45. Quinn Grundy. "'Whether Something Cool Is Good Enough': The Role of Evidence, Sales Representatives, and Nurses' Expertise in Hospital Purchasing Decisions." *Social Science & Medicine* 165 (2016): 82-91.

46. Oya Eddama and Joanna Coast. "A Systematic Review of the Use of Eco-

nomic Evaluation in Local Decision-Making." *Health Policy* 86, nos. 2–3 (2008): 129–41.

47. Oya Eddama and Joanna Coast. "Use of Economic Evaluation in Local Health Care Decision-Making in England: A Qualitative Investigation." *Health Policy* 89, no. 3 (2009): 261–70.

48. Sarah Wadmann. "Physician-Industry Collaboration: Conflicts of Interest and the Imputation of Motive." *Social Studies of Science* 44, no. 4 (2014): 531–54.

49. Dana Katz, Arthur L. Caplan, and John F. Merz. "All Gifts Large and Small: Toward an Understanding of the Ethics of Pharmaceutical Industry Gift Giving." *American Journal of Bioethics* 10, no. (2010): 11–17.

50. Anna Gorman. "The Rise of Specialist Sepsis Nurses to Help Hospitals Coordinate Treatment." *MedCity News*, June 21, 2017, http://medcitynews .com/2017/06/the-rise-of-sepsis-nurses-at-hospitals/.

51. Annemarie Jutel and David B. Menkes. "Soft Targets: Nurses and the Pharmaceutical Industry." *PLoS Medicine* 5, no. 2 (2008): e5.

52. Martin Woods. "Nursing Ethics Education: Are We Really Delivering the Good(s)?" *Nursing Ethics* 12, no. 1 (2005): 5–18.

INDEX

academic medical centers, 5, 14, 23-24, 52, 69, 71, 111

accountability, 114, 115, 135

advertising, 28, 57, 71, 116, 118-19

Affordable Care Act, 5

alarm fatigue, 92-94

ambulance companies, 140-41

American Association of Critical Care Nurses (AACN), 57, 89

Association of periOperative Registered Nurses, 11

Australia, 9, 132, 139

bargaining, 111-15, 118, 126; nurses' tactics and strategies in, 113-14, 115

bias, 7, 43, 99, 127, 139; in decision making, 116, 118-19, 136; and disclosure, 133-34

black box warning, 7

brand loyalty, 24

break rooms, 24, 48-49, 110, 141

cardiac catheterization lab, 13-14, 38-39, 69, 134, 138

Centers for Medicare and Medicaid Services, 5, 49, 134

clinical nurse specialists, 41, 52-53, 62, 63, 85-87, 90-91, 116, 148-49

clinical trials, 7, 146

Code of Ethics for Nurses, 101, 128

codes of conduct, 73, 78, 138

cold calls, 17, 37, 39, 53-54, 128, 146. *See also* drop-in sales visits

conferences, 11, 62, 69-71, 89, 98, 120, 130, 138, 141, 147. *See also* expos and trade shows

conflicts of interest, 78, 102, 120-21, 124-25, 128, 133; hospital policies on,

14, 19, 71, 104, 128; measures needed to address, 136, 145, 147-49

consultants, 25, 140; nurses as, 69, 71, 78, 130, 132; physicians as, 8, 71-72

Consumer Products Report, 145-46

continuing education, 17, 105, 140, 141; need for in-house, 148-49; outsourcing of, 56, 58

Critical Care Expo, 13, 69

dependence, 56, 105, 117; relationships of, 95-96, 97

dialysis, 86-87, 95-97

disclosure, 71, 120, 147, 148; need to move beyond, 133-37; and nurses, 78-79, 104, 132; and Sunshine Act, 6, 133

doctor's orders, 10, 19, 82, 131; workarounds for, 91-92, 94

drop-in sales visits, 30, 41, 104. *See also* cold calls

education: debunking industry's role in, 133, 137-40; marketing function of, 15-16, 45-55, 138; outsourcing of, 137-38. *See also* continuing education; in-servicing

electronic health record, 24-25

emergency department, 74, 82, 86, 92

evidence-based decisions, 40, 93, 127, 146-47

expos and trade shows, 11, 13, 57, 69, 73-74, 84-86, 98

false economies, 137-38, 139-40

favoritism, 124-25

Federal Anti-Kickback Statute, 138

Food and Drug Administration, 114

France, 7, 132
Freidson, Eliot, 142
friendship, 63-64, 69-70, 77-78; by design, 60-62; sales reps as "perfect friends," 19, 55, 56, 59-60, 61, 66, 119, 125-26

gabapentin, 8
GE Healthcare, 89-90
gifts, 60, 77, 127, 140-41, 150; "educational" vs. "entertainment," 62, 138; physicians as recipients of, 5-6, 139, 150; policies prohibiting, 104, 110, 147, 148
Grassley, Charles, 6, 9

healthcare system, 143, 149; corporatization and commercialization of, 132-33, 140-44; cost pressures facing, 17, 75; power dynamics within, 98, 102, 131; and public trust, 22, 144-45, 149-50
Hospira, 57-58
hospitals: budgets of, 12, 15, 28, 36, 58, 73-74, 111; conflict of interest policies of, 14, 71, 104, 128; cost-control, 56, 91, 95, 105, 140; and credentialing companies, 30; disclosure policies of, 71, 104; employment of nurses by, 58, 102, 142; for-profit and not-for-profit, 140; gift prohibitions by, 104, 110; official roles to sales reps at, 5, 7, 16-17, 55-56, 68, 69, 128, 130-31, 134-35; outsourcing to industry by, 56, 58-59, 78, 137-38; power relations within, 98, 102, 131; purchasing committees of, 11-12, 28, 34-44, 52-53, 66, 77, 104, 124-25, 146; relationships with industry encouraged by, 12, 27, 55-56, 66-67
"human factors," 73-77

incentive realignment, 148-49
infection control specialty, 48, 50, 103, 121, 123-24
in-servicing, 14, 50, 65-66; and nursing care, 45-46, 48; and sales, 46, 51-53,

54-55. *See also* education; product support
"insiders," 71-73, 75-77, 131
intensive care unit (ICU), 31, 52-53, 70, 85-86; culture of, 98-99, 100
invisibility: of nurse-industry interactions, 20, 27, 87-88, 130-31; of nurses and nursing work, 58, 85, 87, 101-2

Joint Commission on Accreditation of Healthcare Organizations, 29, 49, 92

key opinion leaders, 71, 75

licensing boards, 147, 148
love-hate relationships, 56, 105

marketing, 24, 87, 102, 127; and education, 15-16, 45-55, 117, 138; experience of, 16, 20, 56, 85, 97-98, 100; explicit and transparent, 146; illegal practices of, 7-8; inclusive nature of, 9, 102, 127, 132; in-service training as tool for, 46, 51-52, 54-55, 117; nurses as target of, 11-12; nurses' view of, 81, 97-98, 127, 128; and purchasing process, 28, 37-38, 43-44, 66, 75, 104; sales reps' strategies for, 16-17, 41-43, 46, 51-52, 54-56, 75, 85, 126-27; and service, 55-56, 149, 150. *See also* nurse-industry interactions; sales representatives
medical device industry, 10, 12, 134, 137
medically related industry: boundaries between support and sales by, 148, 149, 150; debunking educational role of, 133, 137-40; defined, 9-10; disclosure of health professionals' ties to, 79, 134, 150; and healthcare, 22, 133, 144; targeting of nurses by, 10-11, 12, 56, 58, 81, 83-84, 85, 87, 140-41; and unions, 143. *See also* medical device industry; nurse-industry interactions; pharmaceutical industry; sales representatives
medical-surgical specialty, 48, 116; and purchasing, 75, 92

Medicare and Medicaid, 59, 147
Merck, 7

National Patient Safety Goals, 92
National Teaching Institute, 57, 89
Newton-Wellesley Hospital, 143
New York Times, 6
nurse-industry interactions: ambivalence about, 21, 56, 64, 105, 116; bargaining in, 111-15, 118, 126; denying existence of, 13-16, 23, 27-28, 82; divergent goals in, 25, 46; ethical aspects of, 106, 120-21, 128-29; experience of, 16, 20, 56, 79, 85, 97-98, 100, 102, 131; and friendships, 59-62, 63-64, 69-70, 77-79, 125-26; "gut feelings" about, 21, 105-6, 115-16, 122, 126, 128; and hospital outsourcing, 56, 58-59, 78, 137-38; and hospital policies, 103-4, 130-31; and in-servicing, 15, 52-53, 66-67; invisibility of, 20, 27, 79, 87-88, 130-31; lack of preparation for, 120, 128-29, 149; as love-hate relationship, 56, 105; minimal oversight of, 16, 18; normalization of, 127, 128, 132-33; policing of, 107-11; policy proposals for, 21-22, 144-49; in purchasing process, 11-12, 37-39, 41; and restaurant dinners, 23-24, 79-80, 83-84, 118, 139; "rules of engagement" in, 20-21, 103, 105-6, 121, 125, 131; sense of threat in, 126-27; structural limits needed for, 127-28, 136-37, 145-47; Sunshine Act omission of, 8-9, 10, 82, 131; transparency and, 78-79, 133-37; vigilance in, 121-26. *See also* sales representatives
nurse managers, 11, 28, 30, 35, 100; as position, 111-12, 149; and sales reps, 33, 34, 41, 51-52, 60, 61, 73, 110
nurses and nursing profession: "as-if" myths around, 82-83, 88-90, 97-98, 100, 102; bargaining by, 111-15, 118, 126; break rooms of, 24, 48-49, 110, 141; Code of Ethics for, 101, 128; as consultants, 69, 71, 78, 130, 132; and disclosure, 78-79, 104, 132; emergency-room, 82; as fastest-growing profession, 9; as gatekeepers, 21, 24, 34, 37, 51, 58, 121-22, 123-24; hospitals' employment of, 58, 102, 142; influence of, 15, 81-83, 84-85, 88-90, 101; and in-services, 46-50; as "insiders," 71-73, 75-77, 131; invisibility of, 58, 85, 102; and "just nurses" myth, 10-12, 82, 131; as paid speakers, 15, 62, 130, 132; as patient advocates, 20, 102, 143, 150; and physicians, 98-99, 131, 142; preparation for industry interactions, 120, 128-29, 149; and purchase orders, 86-87; and purchasing committees, 14, 15, 35, 36-39, 52-53, 66, 124-25; recognition and respect for, 97-100, 131; skepticism toward industry by, 115-21; and treatment decisions, 80-83, 81-83, 84-88, 101-2; undervaluing of, 100, 101; unions of, 142-43; and work-arounds, 90-97, 131; and "working-in-between," 142

off-label use, 7-8
Open Payments database, 5-6, 133, 134, 145
operating room, 21, 35, 74; sales reps in, 1-4, 12, 16, 31-33, 59, 107-8, 111, 135-36, 148
opioid crisis, 8
outsourcing to industry, 20, 56, 59, 74, 78; of education tasks, 56, 58, 137-38
oversight: of industry interactions, 16, 18, 138

paranoia, 21, 115-17, 118, 120
patient monitoring, 91, 92, 94
patient safety, 92, 94; "enhancing," 29, 57-58; nurses' concern about, 29, 115, 121, 126
pharmaceutical industry, 23-24, 62, 75, 83-84, 137; consultants for, 8, 69, 71-72, 130; marketing strategies of, 7-8, 9, 24, 138. *See also* medically related industry

treatment decisions, 81-83, 84-85
trust, 6, 105, 124; public, 22, 144-45, 149-50

unions, 142-43

vendor credentialing, 28-34
Vendor Credentialing Service (VCS),
    29-30

vigilance, 121-26
Vioxx, 7

Warner-Lambert, 8
work-arounds, 90-97, 131
"working in-between," 142
wound care, 41, 42-43, 63-66, 91,
    117-18